Healthy

Low Fodmap

Cookbook

TRANSFORM YOUR DIET WITH GUT-FRIENDLY AND DELICIOUS RECIPES TO IMPROVE YOUR IBS AND ACHIEVE OPTIMAL DIGESTIVE HEALTH

ROSEMARIE WATKINS

DEDICATION

This cookbook is dedicated to all those who have struggled with digestive issues and know the frustration of limited food choices. May these recipes bring joy and flavor back into your life and empower you to take control of your health. Remember, every sm all step towards a healthier lifestyle is a victory worth celebrating. Cheers to delicious and nutritious meals, made with love and care.   .

Table of Contents

INTRODUCTION 14

The Low Fodmap Concept... 14

Benefits for people suffering from IBS and other digestive ailments.... 15

What is the most common Fodmap Triggers................................ 18

How to know if low fodmap diet is working 19

What foods are permitted and which should be avoided...................21

Meal Planning and Preparation for Low-FODMAP Diets 23

Meal planning and preparation advice and techniques.................... 24

Low Fodmap Breakfast 34

Low Fodmap Breakfast Smoothie Bowl.................................... 35

Low Fodmap Breakfast Quinoa Bowl 36

Low Fodmap Breakfast Avocado Toast 37

Low Fodmap Breakfast Omelet 38

Low Fodmap Breakfast Yogurt Parfait 39

Low Fodmap Breakfast Scrambled Tofu 40

Low Fodmap Breakfast Egg and Sausage Breakfast Tacos 41

Low Fodmap Breakfast Apple and Oat Porridge.......................... 42

Low Fodmap Breakfast Oat and Banana Muffins 43

Low Fodmap Breakfast Blueberry and Almond Pancakes 44

Low Fodmap Breakfast Egg and Vegetable Frittata 45

Low Fodmap Breakfast Burrito 46

Low Fodmap Breakfast Banana and Peanut Butter Oatmeal 47

Low Fodmap Breakfast Sausage and Egg Sandwich 48

Low Fodmap Breakfast Salad 49

Low Fodmap Breakfast Stuffed Sweet Potato 50

Low Fodmap Breakfast Smoothie..51

Low Fodmap Breakfast Quinoa Bowl 52

Low Fodmap Breakfast Fried Rice 53

Low Fodmap Breakfast Polenta and Egg 54

Low Fodmap Breakfast Tofu Scramble 55

Low Fodmap Breakfast Avocado Toast 56

Low Fodmap Breakfast Yogurt Parfait 57

Low Fodmap Breakfast Scrambled Eggs and Bacon 58

Low Fodmap Breakfast Hash 59

Low Fodmap Breakfast Omelette 60

Low Fodmap Breakfast Oatmeal Muffins 61

Low Fodmap Breakfast Yogurt with Berries and Granola 62

Low Fodmap Breakfast Frittata 63

Low Fodmap Lunch 64

Quinoa and Black Bean Salad..65

Lettuce Wraps with Chicken and Mango 66

Spinach and Feta Stuffed Chicken 67

Grilled Portobello Mushroom Burgers 68

Zucchini Noodle Pasta 69

Cucumber and Avocado Sushi Rolls 70

Coconut Curry Soup 71

Garlic and Lemon Shrimp Skewers............................ 72

Tuna Salad Lettuce Wraps.. 73

Stuffed Bell Peppers 74

Roasted Eggplant and Tomato Pasta 75

Pesto and Tomato Grilled Cheese Sandwich 76

Green Salad with Lemon Vinaigrette 77

Sesame Tofu Stir Fry 78

Cobb Salad with Grilled Chicken 79

Spicy Black Bean and Sweet Potato Tacos................. 80

Lemon and Herb Grilled Chicken 81

Creamy Tomato and Basil Soup 82

Pork and Apple Skewers.. 83

Spinach and Feta Stuffed Chicken Breasts 84

Lemon and Herb Quinoa Salad 85

Cauliflower Fried Rice 86

Lentil and Vegetable Stew 87

Beef and Broccoli Stir Fry 88

Creamy Garlic and Mushroom Chicken 89

Stuffed Zucchini Boats 90

Tuna Salad Lettuce Wraps.. 92

Grilled Eggplant and Mozzarella Sandwiches 93

Spinach and Ricotta Stuffed Shells 94

Pesto Chicken and Vegetable Skewers........................ 95

Low Fodmap Dinner 96

Creamy Chicken and Mushroom Pasta 97

Grilled Salmon with Lemon and Herb 98

Slow Cooker Beef Stew 99

Spinach and Feta Stuffed Pork Tenderloin 100

Shrimp and Broccoli Stir Fry 101

Creamy Tomato and Basil Soup 102

Lemon and Herb Roasted Chicken 103

Crispy Baked Chicken Tenders 104

Slow Cooker BBQ Pulled Pork 105

Spaghetti Bolognese 106

Garlic and Herb Grilled Vegetables 107

Potato and Leek Soup 108

Baked Eggplant Parmesan 109

Lemon and Herb Grilled Salmon 110

Meatloaf 111

Black Bean and Sweet Potato Enchiladas 112

Baked Cod with Tomatoes and Capers 113

Pan-Seared Scallops with Lemon Butter Sauce 114

Chicken Parmesan 115

Turkey and Vegetable Meatballs 116

Spinach and Feta Stuffed Chicken 117

Lentil and Vegetable Soup 118

Shrimp and Vegetable Skewers 119

Vegetable and Tofu Stir Fry 120

Grilled Eggplant and Tomato Stack 121

Low Fodmap Vegetarian 122

Spinach and feta stuffed portobello mushrooms 123

Zucchini noodles with avocado pesto 124

Eggplant rollatini 125

Sweet potato and black bean enchiladas 126

Quinoa and black bean burgers 127

Cauliflower and chickpea curry 128

Lentil and spinach lasagna 129

Stuffed bell peppers... 130

Tofu and vegetable stir-fry 131

Chickpea and spinach curry 132

Black bean and sweet potato tacos 133

Roasted vegetable and quinoa salad 134

Lentil and vegetable shepherd's pie 135

Spaghetti Squash and Pesto 136

Vegetable and bean chili 137

Quinoa and vegetable Buddha bowl...138

Vegetable and lentil curry 139

Vegetable and tofu curry 140

Vegetable and chickpea curry 141

Eggplant and tomato parmesan 142

Vegetable and paneer curry 143

Vegetable and bean enchiladas 144

Vegetable and tofu stir fry 145

Vegetable and cashew curry 146

Vegetable and quinoa casserole 147

Vegetable and seitan curry 148

Vegetable and tempeh chili...149

Low Fodmap Sides Dishes 150

Roasted Vegetables 151

Quinoa Salad 152

Cauliflower Rice 153

Garlic-Infused Mashed Potatoes 154

Green Beans with Lemon and Almonds 155

Baked Sweet Potato Fries......................................156

Grilled Asparagus 157

Cabbage Slaw 158

Roasted Brussels Sprouts 159

Carrot and Ginger Puree 160

Lemon and Herb Grilled Fish 161

Baked Zucchini Fries 162

Pan-Fried Radicchio 163

Creamed Spinach 164

Low Fodmap Dessert 165

Blueberry Crumble..167

Chocolate Mousse 168

Apple Crisp 169

Lemon Bars..170

Chocolate Chip Cookies......................................171

Strawberry Sorbet 172

Rice Pudding 173

Chocolate Pudding 174

Peach Cobbler 175

Banana Bread 176

Mango Sorbet 177

Tapioca Pudding 178

Brownies 179

Pecan Pie 180

Pineapple Upside-Down Cake 181

Conclusion 183

Disclaimer Notice:

Please note the information contained within this document is for educational and entertainment purposes only. All effort   has been executed to present accurate, up to date, and reliable, complete information. No warranties of any kind are declared or implied. Readers acknowledge that the author is not engaging in the rendering of legal, financial, medical or professional advi   ce. The content within this book has been derived from various sources. Please consult a licensed professional before attempting any techniques outlined in this book.

By reading this document, the reader agrees that under no circumstances is the author res ponsible for any losses, direct or indirect, which are incurred as a result of the use of the information contained within this document, including, but not limited to,   — errors, omissions, or inaccuracies.

ABOUT THE AUTHOR

The author of The Low Fodmap Cookbook is a passionate advocate for healthy living and empowering individuals to take control of their health. With years of experience in the health and wellness industry, the author has witnessed firsthand the transformative power of good nutrition on overall health and wellbeing.

Driven by a deep desire to help others, the author has dedicated countless hours to researching and developing delicious and nutritious low Fodmap recipes that can help those with digestive sensitivities live their best lives. Through tireless effort and hard work, the author has created a comprehensive guide that not only provides delicious recipes but also educates readers on the benefits of the low Fodmap diet and how to make it a sustainable lifestyle.

With a hope that everyone can experience the joy and freedom that comes with a healthy and nourishing diet, the author pours their heart and soul into every recipe and word in this book. From the author's passion for helping others to their unwavering dedication to creating a healthier world, this cookbook is a true testament to the power of hard work, hope, and the desire to make a difference.

INTRODUCTION

THE LOW FODMAP CONCEPT

Low Fodmap cooking is a specific approach to cooking and eating that is intended to assist people suffering from IBS and other digestive problems in managing their symptoms and improve their overall health. The Low Fodmap diet is built around Fodmaps, a type of short-chain carbohydrate that is poorly absorbed in the small intestine. These carbohydrates can ferment in the intestine, causing gas, bloating, abdominal discomfort, and other IBS symptoms.

The Low Fodmap diet is intended to limit Fodmap consumption while minimizing the stomach's fermentation. Typically, the diet is separated into two phases: elimination and reintroduction. During the elimination phase, all high Fodmap items are removed from the diet, leaving only low Fodmap meals. This stage usually lasts 6-8 weeks to identify any items that may be triggering discomfort.

The reintroduction step begins once the elimination phase is done. High Fodmap foods are progressively reintroduced into the diet during this phase, and symptoms are observed to identify which foods can and cannot be tolerated. This approach assists individuals in determining their Fodmap threshold, or the amount of Fodmaps they can handle without having symptoms.

The Low Fodmap diet is challenging but an excellent strategy for managing IBS and other digestive issues. Individuals who follow the Low Fodmap diet can lessen their symptoms, enhance their quality of life, and reach maximum health.

Low Fodmap cooking entails using low Fodmap components, replacing high Fodmap items with low Fodmap alternatives, and employing cooking procedures that reduce Fodmap fermentation in the gut. Low Fodmap dishes are tasty and simple to make and may be used for breakfast, lunch, and supper, as well as snacks and desserts.

Ingredients with a low Fodmap rating include:

The fruits include berries, oranges, lemons, limes, kiwis, and passionfruit. The vegetables include leafy greens, broccoli, Bok choy, carrot, and zucchini. Chicken, fish, turkey, and lean cuts of beef and hog are all good protein sources.

Grains include rice, quinoa, oats, gluten-free breads, and pastas. Lentils, chickpeas, and black beans are examples of legumes.

The following high Fodmap substances should be avoided:

Apples, apricots, mango, pears, and watermelon are among the fruits.

Garlic, onion, leeks, and cauliflower are among the vegetables.

Dairy products include milk, yogurt, and soft cheeses.

Lentils, chickpeas, and black beans are examples of legumes.

Furthermore, keep in mind that the Low Fodmap diet may not be suited for everyone. Some people may have underlying medical issues that make diet compliance difficult, such as malabsorption or food allergies. Before beginning any new food plan, it is critical to contact with a healthcare expert.

BENEFITS FOR PEOPLE SUFFERING FROM IBS AND OTHER DIGESTIVE AILMENTS

Reducing IBS Symptoms

One of the main advantages of the Low Fodmap diet is that it can help to lessen IBS symptoms such as bloating, gas, abdominal discomfort, and diarrhea. Individuals with IBS can lessen fermentation in the gut and reduce symptoms by avoiding high Fodmap meals and ingesting only low Fodmap foods.

Improving Quality of Life

The Low Fodmap diet can also assist people with IBS and other digestive issues improve their quality of life. Individuals can feel better and enjoy life more completely by minimizing symptoms and obtaining optimal health.

Optimal Health

The Low Fodmap diet is not only useful for those with IBS and other digestive diseases, but it can also assist people who don't have these conditions attain optimal health. Individuals can enhance their general health and well -being by eating a well -balanced diet high in nutrients and low in Fodmaps.

Identifying Food Triggers

The Low Fodmap diet can also aid in the identification of personal food triggers. Individuals can identify which foods they can tolerate and which foods they sh ould avoid by removing high Fodmap meals and gradually reintroducing them.

Simple to Follow

The Low Fodmap diet is simple to follow, and there are many Low Fodmap alternatives available. On the market, people may discover a broad range of Low Fodmap recipe s, components, and goods.

Weight Loss

Following the Low Fodmap diet may cause some people to lose weight. This is frequently due to their use of more nutrient -dense meals while avoiding high -calorie, high -Fodmap items.

Improving digestion

The Low Fodmap d iet can also aid in digestion by decreasing fermentation in the stomach and improving nutrient absorption. This can result in higher nutritional status and general wellness.

Improving gut health

The Low Fodmap diet can assist to enhance gut health by lowe ring inflammation and encouraging the development of good bacteria. This can result in a healthier gut microbiota and overall greater health.

Inflammation reduction

The Low Fodmap diet can also aid in the reduction of inflammation in the stomach and throughout the body. This can result in better overall health and a lower risk of chronic illnesses.

Improving mental health

The Low Fodmap diet can assist improve mental health by lowering anxiety and depression symptoms. This might be because the Low Fod map diet can enhance gut health and reduce inflammation, both of which can benefit mental health.

Gluten -free

The Low Fodmap diet is also appropriate for gluten   -free persons. Many gluten   -free Low Fodmap choices are available, and many gluten   -free items ar   e also Low Fodmap.

Possibilities

The Low Fodmap diet provides a wide range of options. Individuals do not have to eat the same thing every day because there are many low Fodmap meals, products, and recipes accessible.

The Science of Fodmaps

FODMAPs are sho   rt -chain carbohydrates that are poorly absorbed in the small intestine. Carbohydrates may be found in a wide range of meals, including fruits, vegetables, cereals, and dairy products.

FODMAPs are digested by gut bacteria in the large intestine, resulting i   n the generation of gas and other byproducts that can induce symptoms such as bloating, abdominal discomfort, and diarrhea in people with irritable bowel syndrome (IBS) or other functional gastrointestinal disorders.

FODMAPs are divided into four groups:

Oligosaccharides are carbohydrates that are composed of short chains of simple sugars, such as fructans and galacto   -oligosaccharides (GOS). They can be found in wheat, onions, garlic, and legumes, among other foods.

Disaccharides are carbohydrates compose   d of two simple sugars, such as lactose, which is present in milk and dairy products.

Monosaccharides are simple sugars like fructose that may be found in fruits, honey, and high fructose corn syrup.

Polyols are sugar alcohols like xylitol and mannitol tha   t may be found in meals like fruits and vegetables, as well as sugar   -free gum and sweets.

It usually consists of three stages:

The elimination phase, during which high FODMAP items are eliminated from the diet for a period of several weeks.

The reintroduct   ion phase involves progressively reintroducing high FODMAP meals one at a time to establish whether individual FODMAPs are causing symptoms.

The customization phase, during which the individual collaborates with a healthcare expert to develop a long   -term,   individualized diet that incorporates as many high FODMAP foods as feasible while maintaining controlling symptoms.

It is critical to emphasize that a low FODMAP diet should only be followed under the supervision of a healthcare expert, since it has the po   tential to cause nutritional deficiencies if not carefully planned and performed.

WHAT IS THE MOST COMMON FODMAP TRIGGERS

Fermentable Oligosaccharides, Disaccharides, Monosaccharides, and Polyols are abbreviated as Fodmap. These are carbohydrate kinds that might induce digestive pain in those who have particular medical disorders, such as Irritable Bowel Syndrome (IBS). In this ebook, we'll go through the most frequent Fodmap triggers and how to deal with them.

Understanding Fodmap Triggers

Among the most popular Fodmap triggers are:

Fructose: A form of sugar that can be found in fruits, honey, and high-fructose corn syrup.

Lactose is a sugar that is present in milk and dairy products.

Fructans are a kind of carbohydrate that may be found in wheat, garlic, and onions.

Galactans are a kind of carbohydrate that may be found in legumes such as beans and lentils.

Polyols: These are carbohydrate molecules present in artificial sweeteners such as xylitol and sorbitol.

Managing Triggers in Fodmap

A low -Fodmap diet is the best method to handle Fodmap triggers. This entails avoiding meals rich in Fodmap carbs. A certified dietician can assist you in developing a customized food plan that includes   low -Fodmap alternatives.

It's also worth noting that everyone's tolerance for Fodmap meals varies. What causes symptoms in one individual may not cause symptoms in another. A food diary is suggested to note which foods trigger symptoms and which do not.

It is also critical to consult with a medical practitioner to rule out any other underlying medical disorders that may be affecting your symptoms.

Fructose, lactose, fructans, galactans, and polyols are the most prevalent Fodmap triggers. Following a low   -Fod map diet and working with a certified dietitian to build a tailored meal plan is the best strategy to manage Fodmap triggers. It's also critical to keep a food diary and consult with a doctor to rule out any other underlying medical concerns.

HOW TO KNOW IF LOW FODMAP DIET IS WORKING

The following tests can be used to see if a low FODMAP diet is effective:

Maintain a food diary: Keep track of what you consume, any symptoms you have, and the intensity of those symptoms. This can assist you in determining which foods are producing issues and which are not.

Take note of your symptoms: Observe any changes in your symptoms, such as bloating, gas, constipation, or diarrhea. If you notice that your symptoms improve or disappear while on the low FODMAP diet, it is quite probable that it is working for you.

Consult a dietitian: A dietitian can assist you in developing a low FODMAP diet plan that matches your specific needs, as well as evaluate your progress and make modifications as required.

Consider the following br   eath test: If you're still not sure, consider getting a breath test to see if your symptoms are caused by small intestine bacterial overgrowth (SIBO).

It's essential to note that some people may not see any improvement in symptoms until several weeks into   the low FODMAP diet, so it may be beneficial to persist with the diet for a while before deciding if it's working for you.

WHAT FOODS ARE PERMITTED AND WHICH SHOULD BE AVOIDED.

A low FODMAP diet often allows the following foods:

Meat, poultry, fish, and e   ggs are all examples of animal products.

Quinoa, rice, and corn are gluten   -free grains.

Bananas, blueberries, and grapes are examples of fruits.

Lettuce, zucchini, and carrots are examples of vegetables.

Almond milk and soy milk are low FODMAP dairy replac   ements.

Lentils, chickpeas, and borlotti beans are examples of well   -tolerated legumes.

Almonds, macadamias, and pumpkin seeds are examples of nuts and seeds.

The following foods should be avoided on a low FODMAP diet:

Fruits high in FODMAPs include apples,   apricots, peaches, and pears.

Asparagus, artichokes, and mushrooms are examples of high FODMAP veggies.

Wheat, barley, and rye are examples of high FODMAP grains.

Dairy items high in FODMAPs, such as milk, yogurt, and ice cream

Lentils,   chickpeas, and borlotti beans are examples of high FODMAP legumes.

Sweeteners rich in FODMAPs, such as honey and high fructose corn syrup

Cashews, pistachios, and sesame seeds are examples of high FODMAP nuts and seeds.

When it comes to low FODMAP cooking,   it's crucial to focus on using naturally low FODMAP items and to restrict the usage of high FODMAP ingredients.

Here are some low FODMAP cooking tips:

Instead of wheat, barley, and rye, try gluten   -free grains like quinoa, rice, and maize.

Instead of cow'   s milk, try low FODMAP dairy substitutes like almond milk, soy milk, or coconut milk.

Instead of raw garlic, which is rich in FODMAPs, use garlic   -infused oil.

Instead of honey or high fructose corn syrup, use low FODMAP sweeteners like maple syrup or Stevia.

Avoid high FODMAP fruits and vegetables like asparagus, artichokes, and mushrooms in favor of low FODMAP choices like lettuce, zucchini, and carrots.

Avoid canned or processed foods that may include high FODMAP components like inulin or high fructose corn syrup.

When eating high FODMAP meals, keep portion amounts in mind. Smaller servings might assist to alleviate discomfort.

If not correctly planned and implemented, it has the potential to result in nutritional shortages. It might be difficult to stick to a low FODMAP diet, but with the advice of a healthcare expert and by experimenting with different low FODMAP components, it is possible to produce delicious and nutritious meals that help control symptoms.

Meal planning and preparation are also crucial aspects of low FODMAP cooking. It's a good idea to plan ahead of time and create a list of low FODMAP products to include in your meals. This will make it simpler to stick to the diet and guarantee that you have the necessary items on hand at all times. Meal preparing and bulk cooking can also be beneficial since they allow you to have low FODMAP meals ready to go when you need them.

It might be difficult to locate low FODMAP choices while dining out. It's a good idea to research restaurants ahead of time and have a list of low FODMAP dishes on hand to order. To satisfy dietary requirements, many restaurants will be ready to offer substitutes or changes to their menu items. If a restaurant does not provide low FODMAP alternatives, it is recommended to avoid it and locate another restaurant that can meet your needs.

In addition to preparing low FODMAP meals at home, you should be cautious of the snacks and beverages you eat. Many processed foods and drinks include high FODMAP components, so choose low FODMAP snacks like rice cakes, plain popcorn, and veggies with hummus instead. Water is usually a safe bet when it comes to drinks, but you may also try herbal tea or caffeine-free coffee.

In conclusion, planning ahead and meal preparing might be beneficial, as can being conscious of the snacks and beverages you eat.

The necessity of meal planning and preparation when following a Low Fodmap diet will be discussed in the next chapter. We will teach meal planning and preparation techniques and methods, such as how to equip your kitchen with Low Fodmap items, how to read food labels, and how to create alternatives for high Fodmap meals. We will also provide a selection of Low Fodmap meals for breakfast, lunch, and supper, as well as snacks and desserts. These dishes are intended to be delicious and simple to make, and they will assist readers in getting started on their Low Fodmap journey. We'll go through how to plan your meals ahead of time, where to get the necessary products, and how to create your own Low Fodmap meal plan and grocery list.

MEAL PLANNING AND PREPARATION FOR LOW-FODMAP DIETS

Low FODMAP meal planning and preparation are critical components of a low FODMAP diet. This diet might be difficult to follow, but with the appropriate planning and preparation, it is possible to prepare tasty and healthy meals that help control symptoms.

To begin meal planning and preparation, make a list of low FODMAP items that you can incorporate into your meals. This will make it simpler to stick to the diet and guarantee that you have the necessary items on hand at all times. Low FODMAP foods include the following:

Meat, poultry, fish, and eggs are all examples of animal products.

Quinoa, rice, and corn are gluten-free grains.

Bananas, blueberries, and grapes are examples of fruits.

Lettuce, zucchini, and carrots are examples of vegetables.

Almond milk and soy milk are low FODMAP dairy replacements.

It's also vital to plan ahead of time for meals that are simple to prepare. Meal planning and bulk cooking can be beneficial since it allows you to have low FODMAP meals ready to go when you need them. Meals that may be prepared ahead of time include the following:

Grilled chicken or fish with quinoa and roasted veggies as a side

Salad with mixed greens, grilled chicken or tofu, and a FODMAP-friendly dressing

Soup or stew cooked with FODMAP-friendly veggies and a gluten-free grain like rice or quinoa

Snacks and beverages should also be considered while following a low FODMAP diet. Many processed foods and drinks include high FODMAP components, so choose low FODMAP snacks like rice cakes, plain popcorn, and veggies with hummus instead. Water is usually a safe bet when it comes to drinks, but you may also try herbal tea or caffeine-free coffee.

Finally, low FODMAP meal planning and preparation are critical for adhering to a low FODMAP diet. It is feasible to produce enjoyable and healthy meals that help control symptoms by making a list of low FODMAP foods, planning for easy-to-make meals, and being conscious of snacks and beverages. Remember, this diet should only be followed under the supervision of a healthcare expert.

MEAL PLANNING AND PREPARATION ADVICE AND TECHNIQUES

Make a list of FODMAP-friendly foods: Make a list of low FODMAP items that you can incorporate into your meals. This will make it simpler to stick to the diet and guarantee that you have the necessary items on hand at all times.

Meal preparation: Prepare meals ahead of time and prepare in quantity. This will save you time and make sticking to the low FODMAP diet easier.

Make a plan for leftovers: Make enough food to have leftovers for lunch or supper the next day.

Use low FODMAP substitutes: For high FODMAP ingredients, look for low FODMAP substitutes. Use garlic -infused oil in place of raw garlic, or gluten-free grains like quinoa, rice, and maize in place of wheat, barley, and rye.

Be cautious of portion proportions: When consuming high FODMAP meals, be mindful of portion quantities. Smaller servings might assist to alleviate discomfort.

Maintain simplicity: Concentrate on basic, easy -to-make dishes with few ingredients.

Plan your dining out: Prepare ahead of time by researching restaurants and having a list of low FODMAP items on hand.

Make a shopping list: Create a shopping list based on your food plan. This will assist you in staying on track and avoiding purchasing high FODMAP items.

Be inventive: Experiment with different low FODMAP products and seasonings to add taste to your meals.

Speak with a professional: For help planning and preparing low FODMAP meals, speak with a registered dietitian or other trained healthcare practitioner.

Here is a 30 -day meal plan using the recipes provided, with a variety of options for breakfast, lunch, and dinner:

Week 1:

Day 1:

- Breakfast: Low Fodmap Breakfast Smoothie   Bowl (Recipe   13)

- Lunch: Quinoa and Black Bean Salad (Recipe   48)

- Dinner: Creamy Chicken and Mushroom Pasta (Recipe 8   4)

- Vegetarian: Spinach and feta stuffed portobello mushrooms. (Recipe 120)

- Sides Dishes: Roasted Vegetables. (Recipe 1   41)

Day 2:

- Breakfast: Low Fodmap Breakfast Avocado Toast (Recipe   15)

- Lunch: Lettuce Wraps with Chicken and Mango (Recipe   49)

- Dinner: Grilled Salmon with Lemon and Herb (Recipe 8   5)

- Vegetarian: Zucchini noodles with avocado pesto. (Recipe 11   2)

- Blueberry Crumble. (Recip   e 156)

Day 3:

- Breakfast: Low Fodmap Breakfast Scrambled Tofu (Recipe   18)

- Lunch: Spinach and Feta Stuffed Chicken (Recipe 5   0)

- Dinner: Slow Cooker Beef Stew (Recipe 8   6)

- Vegetarian: Eggplant rollatini (Recipe 1   13)

- Sides Dishes: Quinoa Salad. (Recipe   70)

Day 4 :

- Breakfast: Low Fodmap Breakfast Egg and Sausage Breakfast Tacos (Recipe   19)

- Lunch: Grilled Portobello Mushroom Burgers (Recipe 5   1)

- Dinner: Spinach and Feta Stuffed Pork Tenderloin (Recipe 8   7)

- Vegetarian: Sweet potato and black bean enchiladas. (Recipe 1   14)

- Sides Dishes: Cauliflower Rice. (Recipe 1   43)

Day 5:

- Breakfast: Low Fodmap Breakfast Apple and Oat Porridge (Recipe   20)

- Lunch: Zucchini Noodle Pasta (Recipe 5   2)

- Dinner: Shrimp and Broccoli Stir Fry (Recipe   88)

- Vegetarian: Quinoa and black bean burgers. (Recipe 1 15)

- Sides Dishes: Garlic   -Infused Mashed Potatoes. (Recipe 1   44)

Day 6:

- Breakfast: Low Fodmap Breakfast Oat and Banana Muffins (Recipe   21)

- Lunch: Cucumber and Avocado Sushi Rolls (Recipe   53)

- Dinner: Creamy Tomato and Basil Soup (Recipe   89)

- Chocolate Mousse. (Recipe 1   57)

Day 7:

- Breakfast: Low Fodmap Breakfast Blueberry and Almond Pancakes (Recipe   23)

- Lunch: Coconut Curry Soup (Recipe   54)

- Dinner: Lemon and Herb Roasted Chicken (Recipe 9   0)

- Vegeta rian: Cauliflower and chickpea curry. (Recipe 1   16)

- Sides Dishes: Baked Sweet Potato Fries. (Recipe 168)

Week 2:

Day 8:

- Breakfast: Low Fodmap Breakfast Egg and Vegetable Frittata (Recipe   24)

- Lunch: Garlic and Lemon Shrimp Skewers (Recipe   56)

- Dinner: Crispy   Baked Chicken Tenders (Recipe 9   1)

- Vegetarian: Lentil and spinach lasagna: (Recipe 1   17)

- Apple Crisp. (Recipe 1   58)

Day 9:

- Breakfast: Low Fodmap Breakfast Breakfast Burrito (Recipe 35)

- Lunch: Tuna Salad Lettuce Wraps (Recipe   78)

- Dinner: Slow Cooker BBQ Pulled   Pork (Recipe 9   2)

- Vegetarian: Stuffed bell peppers. (Recipe 1   18)

- Strawberry Sorbet (Recipe 1   61)

Day 10:

- Breakfast: Low Fodmap Breakfast Banana and Peanut Butter Oatmeal (Recipe   27)

- Lunch: Stuffed Bell Peppers (Recipe   118)

- Dinner: Spaghetti   Bolognese (Recipe 9   3)

- Vegetarian: Tofu and vegetable stir   -fry. (Recipe 1 19)

- Sides Dishes: Grilled Asparagus. (Recipe 1   47)

Day 11:

- Breakfast: Low Fodmap Breakfast Sausage and Egg Sandwich (Recipe   28)

- Lunch: Roasted Eggplant and Tomato Pasta (Recipe   59)

- Dinn er: Cauliflower Fried Rice (Recipe   71)

- Vegetarian: Chickpea and spinach curry: (Recipe 12   0)

- Lemon Bars. (Recipe 1   59)

Day 12:

- Breakfast: Low Fodmap Breakfast Salad (Recipe 3   0)

- Lunch: Pesto and Tomato Grilled Cheese Sandwich (Recipe 6   0)

- Dinner: Garlic and He   rb Grilled Vegetables (Recipe 9   4)

- Vegetarian: Black bean and sweet potato tacos. (Recipe 1   21)

- Chocolate Chip Cookies. (Recipe 1   60)

Day 13:

- Breakfast: Low Fodmap Breakfast Stuffed Sweet Potato (Recipe 3   1)

- Lunch: Sesame Tofu Stir Fry (Recipe 6   2)

- Dinner: Pota   to and Leek Soup (Recipe   95)

- Vegetarian: Roasted vegetable and quinoa salad. (Recipe 1   22)

- Rice Pudding. (Recipe 1   62)

Day 14:

- Breakfast: Low Fodmap Breakfast Smoothie (Recipe   32)

- Lunch: Cobb Salad with Grilled Chicken (Recipe 6   3)

- Dinner: Baked   Eggplant Parmesan (Recipe 9   6)

- Vegetarian: Lentil and vegetable shepherd's pie. (Recipe 1   23)

Week 3:

Day 15:

- Breakfast: Low Fodmap Breakfast Quinoa Bowl (Recipe   33)

- Lunch: Spicy Black Bean and Sweet Potato Tacos. (Recipe   65)

- Dinner: Quinoa and Black Bean Sa   lad (Recipe 48)

- Vegetarian: Spaghetti Squash and Pesto. (Recipe 1   24)

- Sides Dishes: Cabbage Slaw. (Recipe 1   48)

Day 16:

- Breakfast: Low Fodmap Breakfast Fried Rice. (Recipe   34)

- Lunch: Lemon and Herb Grilled Chicken. (Recipe   66)

- Dinner: Stuffed Bell Peppers.   (Recipe   118)

- Vegetarian: Vegetable and bean chili (Recipe 1   25)

- Chocolate Pudding. (Recipe 16   3)

Day 17:

- Breakfast: Low Fodmap Breakfast Polenta and Egg. (Recipe 3   5)

- Lunch: Creamy Tomato and Basil Soup. (Recipe   89)

- Dinner: Beef and Broccoli Stir Fry. (Recipe   73)

- Vegetarian: Quinoa and vegetable Buddha bowl (Recipe 1   27)

- Sides Dishes: Roasted Brussels Sprouts. (Recipe 1   49)

Day 18:

- Breakfast: Low Fodmap Breakfast Tofu Scramble. (Recipe   37)

- Lunch: Pork and Apple Skewers. (Recipe   68)

- Dinner: Meatloaf (Recipe   98)

- Vegetarian: Vegetable and lentil curry. (Recipe   128)

- Peach Cobbler (Recipe   164)

Day 19:

- Breakfast: Low Fodmap Breakfast Avocado Toast (Recipe   38)

- Lunch: Spinach and Feta Stuffed Chicken Breasts.   (Recipe   69)

- Dinner: Black Bean and Sweet Potato Enchiladas. (Recipe   99)

- Vegetarian: Vegetable and tofu curry. (Recipe 1   29)

- Sides Dishes: Lemon and He   rb Grilled Fish. (Recipe 1   51)

Day 20:

- Breakfast: Low Fodmap Breakfast Scrambled Eggs and Bacon. (Recipe 4   0)

- Lunch: Cauliflower Fried Rice. (Recipe 7   1)

- Dinner: Baked Cod with Tomatoes and Capers. (Recipe 10   0)

- Vegetarian: Vegetable and chickpea curry. (Recip   e 130)

- Sides Dishes: Carrot and Ginger Puree. (Recipe 1   50)

Day 21:

- Breakfast: Low Fodmap Breakfast Hash. (Recipe 4   2)

- Lunch: Lentil and Vegetable Stew. (Recipe 7   2)

- Dinner: Pan   -Seared Scallops with Lemon Butter Sauce. (Recipe 10   1)

- Vegetarian: Spinach and   feta stuffed portobello mushrooms. (Recipe 1   10)

- Sides Dishes: Lemon and Herb Roasted Chicken. (Recipe   90)

Week 3:

Day 22:

- Breakfast: Low Fodmap Breakfast Omelette. (Recipe 4   3)

- Lunch: Beef and Broccoli Stir Fry. (Recipe 7   3)

- Dinner: Chicken Parmesan. (Recipe   102)

- Vegetarian: Eggplant and tomato parmesan (Recipe 1   31)

- Banana Bread. (Recipe 1   65)

Day 23:

- Breakfast: Low Fodmap Breakfast Oatmeal Muffins. (Recipe 4   4)

- Lunch: Creamy Garlic and Mushroom Chicken. (Recipe 7   4)

- Dinner: Turkey and Vegetable   Meatballs. (Recipe 10   3)

- Vegetarian: Vegetable and paneer curry. (Recipe 1   33)

- Brownies. (Recipe 1   68)

Day 24:

- Breakfast: Low Fodmap Breakfast Yogurt with Berries and Granola. (Recipe   45)

- Lunch: Stuffed Zucchini Boats. (Recipe   76)

- Dinner: Spinach and Feta Stu   ffed Chicken. (Recipe   104)

- Vegetarian: Vegetable and bean enchiladas: (Recipe   134)

- Pineapple Upside   -Down Cake. (Recipe 1   70)

Day 25:

- Breakfast: Low Fodmap Breakfast Frittata. (Recipe   46)

- Lunch: Tuna Salad Lettuce Wraps. (Recipe   78)

- Dinner: Lentil and   Vegetable Soup. (Recipe 1   05)

- Vegetarian: Vegetable and tofu stir fry. (Recipe 13   5)

- Sides Dishes: Baked Zucchini Fries. (Recipe 15   2)

Day 26:

- Breakfast: Low Fodmap Breakfast Burrito. (Recipe 2   5)

- Lunch: Grilled Eggplant and Mozzarella Sandwiches. (Recipe   79)

- Dinner: Shrimp and Vegetable Skewers. (Recipe 114)

- Vegetarian: Vegetable and lentil shepherd's pie. (Recipe 154)

- Sides Dishes: Pan -Fried Radicchio. (Recipe 1   53)

Day 27:

- Breakfast: Low Fodmap Breakfast Quinoa Bowl (Recipe   33)

- Lunch: Spinach and   Ricotta Stuffed Shells. (Recipe 8   1)

- Dinner: Creamy Chicken and Mushroom Pasta. (Recipe   84)

- Vegetarian: Vegetable and cashew curry. (Recipe 1   36)

- Mango Sorbet (Recipe 1   66)

Day 28:

- Breakfast: Low Fodmap Breakfast Egg and Sausage Breakfast Tacos. (Recipe   19)

- L unch: Pesto Chicken and Vegetable Skewers. (Recipe 8   2)

- Dinner: Vegetable and Tofu Stir Fry. (Recipe 1   35)

- Vegetarian: Vegetable and quinoa casserole. (Recipe 1   37)

- Pecan Pie. (Recipe 1   69)

Day 29:

- Breakfast: Low Fodmap Breakfast Sausage and Egg Sandwich (Reci   pe 28)

- Lunch: Roasted Eggplant and Tomato Pasta (Recipe   59)

- Dinner: Cauliflower Fried Rice (Recipe   71)

- Vegetarian: Vegetable and seitan curry. (Recipe 1   38)

- Sides Dishes: Creamed Spinach. (Recipe 1   54)

Day 30:

- Breakfast: Low Fodmap Breakfast Breakfast Burrito (Recipe 35)

- Lunch: Tuna Salad Lettuce Wraps (Recipe   78)

- Dinner: Slow Cooker BBQ Pulled Pork (Recipe 9   2)

- Vegetarian: Vegetable and tempeh chili (Recipe 1   39)

- Tapioca Pudding. (Recipe 1   67)

Low Fodmap Breakf   ast

Welcome to our Low Fodmap Breakfast Cookbook! Here is a compilation of tasty and healthy breakfast recipes ideal for folks on a low Fodmap diet.

Breakfast is the most essential meal of the day, and it may be difficult to find low Fodmap alternatives that are both tasty and enjoyable. That's why we've produced a list of 30 easy and delicious low   -Fodmap breakfast dishes that are sure to satisfy your taste buds. There's something for everyone here, from smoothies and pancakes to frittatas an   d burritos.

All recipes in this cookbook have been carefully created to be low Fodmap and suited for anyone following a low Fodmap diet. Each recipe contains a list of ingredients, step   -by-step directions, and comments on how to make any required alteratio   ns.

We hope you enjoy these wonderful low Fodmap breakfast dishes and that they make your mornings a little bit simpler and a lot more delightful! Happy cooking!

LOW FODMAP BREAKFAST SMOOTHIE BOWL

Made for: Breakfast | Prep Time: 5 minutes | Total time: 5 minutes | Servings: 01 people

Ingredients

- 1 banana
- 1/2 cup frozen berries (strawberries, blueberries, raspberries)
- 1/4 cup almond milk
- 1 tablespoon chia seeds
- 1 tablespoon almond butter
- Toppings: granola, fresh berries, shredded coconut

Instructions

1. In a blender, combine the banana, frozen berries, almond milk, chia seeds, and almond butter.
2. Blend until smooth and creamy.
3. Pour the smoothie into a bowl and top with granola, fresh berries, and shredded coconut.
4. Enjoy immediately.

Notes:

You can use any frozen fruit you prefer for this recipe.

If the smoothie is too thick, add more almond milk until you reach your desired consistency.

LOW FODMAP BREAKFAST QUINOA BOWL

Made for: Breakfast | Prep Time: 5 minutes | Total time: 20 | Servings: 0 1 people

Ingredients

- 1 cup cooked quinoa
- 1/2 cup diced tomatoes
- 1/2 cup diced cucumber
- 1/4 cup diced red onion
- 1/4 cup crumbled feta cheese
- 2 tablespoons chopped parsley
- 1 tablespoon olive oil
- 1 teaspoon lemon juice
- Salt and pepper, to taste

Instructions

1. In a small bowl, combine the olive oil, lemon juice, salt, and pepper.
2. In a large bowl, combine the cooked quinoa, diced tomatoes, cucumber, red onion, and crumbled feta cheese.
3. Drizzle the dressing over the quinoa mixture and toss to combine.
4. Top with chopped parsley, and enjoy immediately.

Notes:

You can use any cooked grain you prefer for this recipe.

If you prefer a warm breakfast, heat the quinoa and vegetables in a pan before adding the dressing and parsley.

LOW FODMAP BREAKFAST AVOCADO TOAST

Made for: Breakfast | Prep Time: 5 minutes | Total time: 5 | Servings: 0 1 people

Ingredients

- 2 slices gluten-free bread
- 1 avocado
- 1/4 teaspoon salt
- 1/4 teaspoon pepper
- 1/4 teaspoon red pepper flakes (optional)
- 1/4 teaspoon lemon juice (optional)

Instructions

1. Toast the bread to your desired level of crispiness.
2. In a small bowl, mash the avocado with a fork.
3. Season the avocado with salt, pepper, red pepper flakes (if using), and lemon juice (if using).
4. Spread the avocado mixture on top of the toasted bread.
5. Enjoy immediately.

Notes:

You can use any bread you prefer for this recipe.

If you're following a strict low Fodmap diet, make sure to use gluten-free bread that is also low Fodmap.

LOW FODMAP BREAKFAST OMELET

Made for: Breakfast | Prep Time: 5 minutes | Total time: 10 | Servings: 0 1 people

Ingredients

- 2 eggs
- 1/4 cup diced bell pepper
- 1/4 cup diced mushrooms
- 1/4 cup diced onion
- 1/4 cup diced tomatoes
- Salt and pepper, to taste
- 1 tablespoon olive oil

Instructions

1. In a small skillet, heat the olive oil over medium heat.
2. Add the bell pepper, mushrooms, onion, and tomatoes to the skillet and sauté for 2-3 minutes until softened.
3. Whisk together the eggs, salt, and pepper in a small bowl.
4. Pour the eggs into the skillet with the vegetables and cook until the eggs are set and lightly browned.
5. Fold the omelet in half and serve immediately.

Notes:

You can use any vegetables you prefer for this recipe.

If you're following a strict low-Fodmap diet, use low-Fodmap vegetables.

LOW FODMAP BREAKFAST YOGURT PARFAIT

Made for: Breakfast | Prep Time: 5 minutes | Total time: 5 | Servings: 0 1 people

Ingredients

- 1/2 cup plain low Fodmap yogurt
- 1/4 cup low Fodmap granola
- 1/4 cup mixed berries (strawberries, blueberries, raspberries)

Instructions

1. Layer the yogurt, granola, and mixed berries in a glass or bowl.
2. Repeat the layers until you reach the top of the glass or bowl.
3. Enjoy immediately.

Notes:

If you're following a strict low Fodmap diet, make sure to use yogurt and granola that are low Fodmap.

LOW FODMAP BREAKFAST SCRAMBLED TOFU

Made for: Breakfast | Prep Time: 5 minutes | Total time: 10 | Servings: 0 1 people

Ingredients

- 1 block of firm tofu
- 1/4 cup diced bell pepper
- 1/4 cup diced mushrooms
- 1/4 cup diced onion
- 1/4 cup diced tomatoes
- 1 tablespoon olive oil
- Salt and pepper, to taste

Instructions

1. In a small skillet, heat the olive oil over medium heat.
2. Crumble the tofu into the skillet and cook for 2-3 minutes until lightly browned.
3. Add the bell pepper, mushrooms, onion, and tomatoes to the skillet and sauté for 2-3 minutes until softened.
4. Season with salt and pepper to taste.

Serve immediately.

LOW FODMAP BREAKFAST EGG AND SAUSAGE BREAKFAST TACOS

Ma de for: Breakfast | *Prep Time: 5 minutes* | *Total time: 10* | *Servings: 0 1 people*

Ingredients

- 2 low Fodmap sausages
- 2 eggs
- 1/4 cup diced bell pepper
- 1/4 cup diced mushrooms
- 1/4 cup diced onion
- 1/4 cup diced tomatoes
- 2 gluten-free or low Fodmap tortillas
- Salt and pepper, to taste
- 1 tablespoon olive oil

Instructions

1. In a small skillet, heat the olive oil over medium heat.
2. Cook the sausages for 2-3 minutes until lightly browned.
3. In a separate skillet, whisk the eggs and scramble until cooked.
4. Add the bell pepper, mushrooms, onion, and tomatoes to the skillet and sauté for 2-3 minutes until softened.
5. Season with salt and pepper to taste.
6. Serve the sausages and eggs in the tortillas and enjoy immediately.

Notes:

If you're following a strict low Fodmap diet, make sure to use sausages and tortillas that are low Fodmap.

LOW FODMAP BREAKFAST APPLE AND OAT PORRIDGE

Made for: Breakfast | *Prep Time: 5 minutes* | *Total time: 10* | *Servings: 0 1 people*

Ingredients

- 1 cup almond milk
- 1/2 cup rolled oats
- 1/2 cup diced apple
- 1 tablespoon honey
- 1 teaspoon cinnamon
- 1/4 teaspoon salt

Instructions

1. In a small saucepan, bring the almond milk to a boil.
2. Add the rolled oats, diced apple, honey, cinnamon, and salt to the saucepan.
3. Reduce the heat to low and let the porridge simmer for 5-7 minutes, or until the oats are cooked, and the apple is tender.
4. Serve immediately and enjoy.

Notes:

If you're following a strict low-Fodmap diet, use low-Fodmap oats.

You can use any milk you prefer for this recipe.

If you prefer a sweeter porridge, you can add more honey to taste.

LOW FODMAP BREAKFAST OAT AND BANANA MUFFINS

Made for: Breakfast | Prep Time: 10 minutes | Total time: 2 5 | Servings: 6 people

Ingredients

- 1 cup gluten-free flour
- 1 cup rolled oats
- 1/2 cup sugar
- 1 teaspoon baking powder
- 1 teaspoon baking soda
- 1 teaspoon cinnamon
- 1/4 teaspoon salt
- 2 ripe bananas
- 2 eggs
- 1/4 cup almond milk
- 1/4 cup melted coconut oil

Instructions

1. Preheat the oven to 350°F.
2. In a large mixing bowl, combine the gluten-free flour, rolled oats, sugar, baking powder, baking soda, cinnamon, and salt.
3. In a separate bowl, mash the bananas with a fork.
4. Add the eggs, almond milk, and melted coconut oil to the mashed bananas and mix until well combined.
5. Add the wet ingredients to the dry ingredients and mix until just combined.
6. Scoop the batter into a muffin tin lined with muffin cups.
7. Bake for 20-25 minutes or until a toothpick inserted into the center comes clean.
8. Let the muffins cool for a few minutes before serving.

LOW FODMAP BREAKFAST BLUEBERRY AND ALMOND PANCAKES

Made for: Breakfast | Prep Time: 5 minutes | Total time: 15 | Servings: 0 4 people

Ingredients

- 1 cup gluten-free flour
- 1 teaspoon baking powder
- 1/4 teaspoon salt
- 1/2 cup almond milk
- 1 egg
- 1/4 cup blueberries
- 1 tablespoon almond butter
- 1 tablespoon honey

Instructions

1. In a large mixing bowl, combine the gluten-free flour, baking powder, and salt.
2. In a separate bowl, whisk together the almond milk and egg.
3. Add the wet ingredients to the dry ingredients and mix until just combined.
4. Fold in the blueberries.
5. Heat a large skillet over medium heat and add a small amount of oil.
6. Using a 1/4 cup measure, pour the batter into the skillet and cook for 2-3 minutes per side or until golden brown.
7. Serve with almond butter and honey on top.

LOW FODMAP BREAKFAST EGG AND VEGETABLE FRITTATA

Made for: Breakfast | Prep Time: 5 minutes | Total time: 20 | Servings: 0 4 people

Ingredients

- 6 eggs
- 1/2 cup diced bell pepper
- 1/2 cup diced mushrooms
- 1/2 cup diced onion
- 1/2 cup diced tomatoes
- Salt and pepper, to taste
- 1 tablespoon olive oil

Instructions

1. In a small skillet, heat the olive oil over medium heat.
2. Add the bell pepper, mushrooms, onion, and tomatoes to the skillet and sauté for 2-3 minutes until softened.
3. Whisk together the eggs, salt, and pepper in a small bowl.
4. Pour the eggs over the vegetables in the skillet and cook for 2-3 minutes or until the edges start to set.
5. Place the skillet under the broiler for 2-3 minutes or until the top is golden brown and the eggs are cooked.
6. Serve immediately.

Notes:

You can use any vegetables you prefer for this recipe.

If you're following a strict low-Fodmap diet, use low-Fodmap vegetables.

LOW FODMAP BREAKFAST BURRITO

Made for: Breakfast | Prep Time: 5 minutes | Total time: 10 | Servings: 0 2 people

Ingredients

- 2 low Fodmap sausages
- 2 eggs
- 1/4 cup diced bell pepper
- 1/4 cup diced mushrooms
- 1/4 cup diced onion
- 1/4 cup diced tomatoes
- 2 gluten-free or low Fodmap tortillas
- Salt and pepper, to taste
- 1 tablespoon olive oil

Instructions

1. In a small skillet, heat the olive oil over medium heat.
2. Cook the sausages for 2-3 minutes until lightly browned.
3. In a separate skillet, whisk the eggs and scramble until cooked.
4. Add the bell pepper, mushrooms, onion, and tomatoes to the skillet and sauté for 2-3 minutes until softened.
5. Season with salt and pepper to taste.
6. Serve the sausages and eggs in the tortillas and enjoy immediately.

Notes:

If you're following a strict low Fodmap diet, make sure to use sausages and tortillas that are low Fodmap.

LOW FODMAP BREAKFAST BANANA AND PEANUT BUTTER OATMEAL

Made for: Breakfast | Prep Time: 5 minutes | Total time: 10 | Servings: 0 1 people

Ingredients

- 1 cup rolled oats
- 1 cup almond milk
- 1 banana
- 1 tablespoon peanut butter
- 1 teaspoon honey
- 1/4 teaspoon cinnamon

Instructions

1. In a small saucepan, bring the almond milk to a boil.
2. Add the rolled oats, banana, peanut butter, honey, and cinnamon to the saucepan.
3. Reduce the heat to low and let the oatmeal simmer for 5-7 minutes until the oats are cooked and the banana is tender.
4. Serve immediately and enjoy.

Notes:

If you're following a strict low Fodmap diet, make sure to use oats that are low Fodmap and peanut butter that is low Fodmap. You can use any milk you prefer for this recipe.

If you prefer sweeter oatmeal, you can add more honey to taste.

LOW FODMAP BREAKFAST SAUSAGE AND EGG SANDWICH

Made for: Breakfast | Prep Time: 5 minutes | Total time: 10 | Servings: 0 1 people

Ingredients

- 2 low Fodmap sausages
- 2 eggs
- 2 slices gluten-free bread
- Salt and pepper, to taste
- 1 tablespoon olive oil

Instructions

1. In a small skillet, heat the olive oil over medium heat.
2. Cook the sausages for 2-3 minutes until lightly browned.
3. In a separate skillet, whisk the eggs and scramble until cooked.
4. Season with salt and pepper to taste.
5. Toast the bread to your desired level of crispiness.
6. Assemble the sandwich with the sausages, eggs, and toasted bread.
7. Enjoy immediately.

Notes:

If you're following a strict low Fodmap diet, make sure to use sausages and bread that are low Fodmap.

LOW FODMAP BREAKFAST SALAD

Made for: Breakfast | Prep Time: 5 minutes | Total time: 5 | Servings: 0 1 people

Ingredients

- 1 cup mixed greens
- 1/4 cup diced tomatoes
- 1/4 cup diced cucumber
- 1/4 cup diced red onion
- 1/4 cup crumbled feta cheese
- 2 tablespoons chopped parsley
- 1 tablespoon olive oil
- 1 teaspoon lemon juice
- Salt and pepper, to taste

Instructions

1. In a small bowl, combine the olive oil, lemon juice, salt, and pepper.
2. In a large bowl, combine the mixed greens, diced tomatoes, cucumber, red onion, and crumbled feta cheese.
3. Drizzle the dressing over the salad and toss to combine.
4. Top with chopped parsley, and enjoy immediately.

Notes:

You can use any mixed greens you prefer for this recipe.

LOW FODMAP BREAKFAST STUFFED SWEET POTATO

Made for: Breakfast | Prep Time: 5 minutes | Total time: 20 | Servings: 0 1 people

Ingredients

- 1 large sweet potato
- 2 eggs
- 1/4 cup diced bell pepper
- 1/4 cup diced mushrooms
- 1/4 cup diced onion
- 1/4 cup diced tomatoes
- Salt and pepper, to taste
- 1 tablespoon olive oil

Instructions

1. Preheat the oven to 375°F.
2. Pierce the sweet potato with a fork and place it in the oven for 20-25 minutes or until it is tender.
3. In a small skillet, heat the olive oil over medium heat.
4. Add the bell pepper, mushrooms, onion, and tomatoes to the skillet and sauté for 2-3 minutes until softened.
5. In a separate skillet, whisk the eggs and scramble until cooked.
6. Season with salt and pepper to taste.
7. Once the sweet potato is cooked, cut it open and stuff it with the sautéed vegetables and scrambled eggs.
8. Serve immediately.

LOW FODMAP BREAKFAST SMOOTHIE

Made for: Breakfast | Prep Time: 5 minutes | Total time: 5 | Servings: 0 1 people

Ingredients

- 1 cup almond milk
- 1 banana
- 1/2 cup mixed berries (strawberries, blueberries, raspberries)
- 1 tablespoon chia seeds
- 1 teaspoon honey

Instructions

1. In a blender, combine the almond milk, banana, mixed berries, chia seeds, and honey.
2. Blend until smooth.
3. Pour into a glass and enjoy immediately.

Notes:

You can use any milk you prefer for this recipe.

If you're following a strict low-Fodmap diet, use low-Fodmap berries.

If you like a sweeter smoothie, you can add more honey to taste.

LOW FODMAP BREAKFAST QUINOA BOWL

Made for: Breakfast | Prep Time: 10 minutes| Total time: 20 | Servings: 0 4 people

Ingredients

- 1 cup quinoa
- 2 cups water
- 1/2 cup diced bell pepper
- 1/2 cup diced mushrooms
- 1/2 cup diced onion
- 1/2 cup diced tomatoes
- 2 tablespoons chopped parsley
- 1 tablespoon olive oil
- Salt and pepper, to taste

Instructions

1. In a small saucepan, bring the quinoa and water to a boil.
2. Reduce the heat to low and let the quinoa simmer for 15-20 minutes until the water is absorbed and the quinoa is cooked.
3. In a small skillet, heat the olive oil over medium heat.
4. Add the bell pepper, mushrooms, onion, and tomatoes to the skillet and sauté for 2-3 minutes until softened.
5. Season with salt and pepper to taste.
6. Once the quinoa is cooked, fluff it with a fork and add the sautéed vegetables.
7. Top with chopped parsley, and enjoy immediately.

LOW FODMAP BREAKFAST FRIED RICE

Made for: Breakfast | Prep Time: 5 minutes | Total time: 20 | Servings: 0 4 people

Ingredients

- 1 cup cooked brown rice
- 1/2 cup diced bell pepper
- 1/2 cup diced mushrooms
- 1/2 cup diced onion
- 1/2 cup diced tomatoes
- 2 eggs
- 2 tablespoons soy sauce
- 1 tablespoon sesame oil
- Salt and pepper, to taste

Instructions

1. In a small skillet, heat the sesame oil over medium heat.
2. Add the bell pepper, mushrooms, onion, and tomatoes to the skillet and sauté for 2-3 minutes until softened.
3. In a separate skillet, whisk the eggs and scramble until cooked.
4. Add the cooked brown rice and soy sauce to the skillet with the vegetables and mix well.
5. Add the scrambled eggs and mix well.
6. Season with salt and pepper to taste.
7. Serve immediately.

LOW FODMAP BREAKFAST POLENTA AND EGG

Made for: Breakfast | Prep Time: 5 minutes | Total time: 20 | Servings: 0 2 people

Ingredients

- 1 cup polenta
- 4 cups water
- 2 eggs
- 1/4 cup grated parmesan cheese
- Salt and pepper, to taste

Instructions

1. In a medium saucepan, bring the water to a boil.
2. Slowly stir in the polenta and reduce the heat to low.
3. Cook for 15-20 minutes, occasionally stirring, until the polenta thickens and is cooked.
4. Remove from heat and stir in the grated parmesan cheese.
5. In a separate skillet, whisk the eggs and scramble until cooked.
6. Season with salt and pepper to taste.
7. Serve the polenta in bowls and top with the scrambled eggs.
8. Enjoy immediately.

LOW FODMAP BREAKFAST TOFU SCRAMBLE

Made for: Breakfast | Prep Time: 5 minutes | Total time: 10 | Servings: 0 4 people

Ingredients

- 1 block of firm tofu
- 1/4 cup diced bell pepper
- 1/4 cup diced mushrooms
- 1/4 cup diced onion
- 1/4 cup diced tomatoes
- 1 tablespoon olive oil
- 1 teaspoon turmeric
- Salt and pepper, to taste

Instructions

1. In a small skillet, heat the olive oil over medium heat.
2. Crumble the tofu with your hands and add it to the skillet.
3. Add the turmeric and sauté for 2-3 minutes until lightly browned.
4. Add the bell pepper, mushrooms, onion, and tomatoes to the skillet and sauté for 2-3 minutes until softened.
5. Season with salt and pepper to taste.
6. Serve immediately.

LOW FODMAP BREAKFAST AVOCADO TOAST

Made for: Breakfast | Prep Time: 5 minutes | Total time: 5 | Servings: 0 2 people

Ingredients

- 2 slices gluten-free bread
- 1 avocado
- Salt and pepper, to taste

Instructions

1. Toast the bread to your desired level of crispiness.
2. Slice the avocado half, remove the pit, and mash it with a fork.
3. Season with salt and pepper to taste.
4. Spread the avocado mash on top of the toasted bread.
5. Enjoy immediately.

LOW FODMAP BREAKFAST YOGURT PARFAIT

Made for: Breakfast | Prep Time: 5 minutes | Total time: 5 | Servings: 0 1 people

Ingredients

- 1 cup low Fodmap yogurt
- 1/2 cup mixed berries (strawberries, blueberries, raspberries)
- 1/4 cup granola (low Fodmap)

Instructions

1. Layer the yogurt, mixed berries, and granola in a tall glass or jar.
2. Repeat the layers until the glass or jar is filled.
3. Enjoy immediately.

LOW FODMAP BREAKFAST SCRAMBLED EGGS AND BACON

Made for: Breakfast | Prep Time: 5 minutes | Total time: 10 | Servings: 0 2 people

Ingredients

- 4 slices soft Fodmap bacon
- 4 eggs
- Salt and pepper, to taste

Instructions

1. In a small skillet, cook the bacon for 2-3 minutes until crispy.
2. Remove the bacon from the skillet and place it on a paper towel to remove the excess grease.
3. In the same skillet, whisk the eggs and scramble until cooked.
4. Season with salt and pepper to taste.
5. Serve the scrambled eggs with the bacon on the side.
6. Enjoy immediately.

LOW FODMAP BREAKFAST HASH

Made for: Breakfast | Prep Time: 10 minutes | Total time: 20 | Servings: 0 2 people

Ingredients

- 1/2 cup diced potatoes
- 1/2 cup chopped bell pepper
- 1/2 cup diced mushrooms
- 1/2 cup diced onion
- 1/2 cup diced tomatoes
- 2 eggs
- 1 tablespoon olive oil
- Salt and pepper, to taste

Instructions

1. In a small skillet, heat the olive oil over medium heat.
2. Add the potatoes, bell pepper, mushrooms, onion, and tomatoes to the skillet and sauté for 10-15 minutes, or until the vegetables are cooked, and the potatoes are crispy.
3. In a separate skillet, whisk the eggs and scramble until cooked.
4. Season with salt and pepper to taste.
5. Serve the hash with the scrambled eggs on top.
6. Enjoy immediately.

LOW FODMAP BREAKFAST OMELETTE

Made for: Breakfast | Prep Time: 5 minutes | Total time: 10 | Servings: 0 2 people

Ingredients

- 4 eggs
- 1/4 cup diced bell pepper
- 1/4 cup diced mushrooms
- 1/4 cup diced onion
- 1/4 cup diced tomatoes
- Salt and pepper, to taste
- 1 tablespoon olive oil

Instructions

1. In a small skillet, heat the olive oil over medium heat.
2. Add the bell pepper, mushrooms, onion, and tomatoes to the skillet and sauté for 2-3 minutes until softened.
3. Whisk together the eggs, salt, and pepper in a small bowl.
4. Pour the eggs over the vegetables in the skillet and cook for 2-3 minutes or until the edges start to set.
5. Use a spatula to flip the omelette and cook for 1-2 minutes on the other side.
6. Serve immediately.

Notes:

You can use any vegetables you prefer for this recipe.

LOW FODMAP BREAKFAST OATMEAL MUFFINS

Made for: Breakfast | Prep Time: 10 minutes | Total time: 30 | Servings: 0 6 people

Ingredients

- 1 cup rolled oats
- 1/2 cup almond flour
- 1/4 cup maple syrup
- 1 egg
- 1/2 cup almond milk
- 1 teaspoon baking powder
- 1 teaspoon vanilla extract
- Salt, to taste

Instructions

1. Preheat the oven to 375°F.
2. In a large mixing bowl, combine the rolled oats, almond flour, maple syrup, egg, almond milk, baking powder, vanilla extract, and salt.
3. Mix well.
4. Grease a muffin tin and spoon the
5. mixture into the muffin cups, filling them about 3/4 of the way full.
6. Bake for 20-25 minutes, or until the muffins are golden brown and a toothpick inserted into the center comes out clean.
7. Let the muffins cool for 5 minutes before removing them from the tin.
8. Serve warm, and enjoy immediately.

LOW FODMAP BREAKFAST YOGURT WITH BERRIES AND GRANOLA

Made for: Breakfast | Prep Time: 5 minutes | Total time: 5 | Servings: 0 1 people

Ingredients

- 1 cup low Fodmap yogurt
- 1/2 cup mixed berries (strawberries, blueberries, raspberries)
- 1/4 cup low Fodmap granola
- 1 teaspoon honey (optional)

Instructions

1. In a bowl, combine the yogurt, mixed berries, and granola.
2. If desired, drizzle honey on top.
3. Enjoy immediately.

Notes:

If you prefer a sweeter yogurt, you can add more honey to taste.

LOW FODMAP BREAKFAST FRITTATA

Made for: Breakfast | Prep Time: 10 minutes | Total time: 30 | Servings: 0 4 people

Ingredients

- 1/2 cup diced bell pepper
- 1/2 cup diced mushrooms
- 1/2 cup diced onion
- 1/2 cup diced tomatoes
- 8 eggs
- 1/4 cup grated parmesan cheese
- 1 tablespoon olive oil
- Salt and pepper, to taste

Instructions

1. Preheat the oven to 375°F.
2. In a small skillet, heat the olive oil over medium heat.
3. Add the bell pepper, mushrooms, onion, and tomatoes to the skillet and sauté for 2-3 minutes until softened.
4. Whisk together the eggs in a large bowl, grated parmesan cheese, salt, and pepper.
5. Add the sautéed vegetables to the egg mixture and mix well.
6. Pour the mixture into a greased 9-inch pie dish.
7. Bake for 20-25 minutes or until the frittata is set and lightly browned on top.
8. Serve immediately.

Low Fodmap Lunch

Eating a low FODMAP diet can be challenging, especially when finding delicious and satisfying lunch options. Many people mistakenly believe that a low FODMAP diet is restrictive and bland. Still, with creativity and the right ingredients, you can enjoy a wide variety of tasty and satisfying meals. In this cookbook, you'll find 30 delicious and easy-to-make low-FODMAP lunch recipes that will help you stick to your diet while still enjoying delicious and satisfying meals. From hearty salads to savory sandwiches, there's something for everyone in this collection of recipes. So, whether you're looking for a quick and easy lunch to take to work or need some inspiration for your next meal, this cookbook has got you covered. Say goodbye to bland and boring meals and hello to flavorful and satisfying low-FODMAP lunch options!

QUINOA AND BLACK BEAN SALAD

Made for: Lunch | Prep Time: 10 minutes | Total time: 20 minutes | Servings: 4-6 people

Ingredients

- 1 cup quinoa
- 1 can black beans (rinsed and drained)
- 1 red bell pepper (diced)
- 1/2 red onion (diced)
- 1/4 cup cilantro (chopped)
- 2 tbsp lime juice
- 1 tbsp olive oil
- salt and pepper to taste

Instructions

1. Cook quinoa according to package instructions.
2. In a large bowl, combine quinoa, black beans, red bell pepper, red onion, cilantro, lime juice, and olive oil.
3. Season with salt and pepper to taste.
4. Serve chilled or at room temperature.

Notes: Make sure to rinse the quinoa thoroughly before cooking to remove saponins, which can cause stomach discomfort.

LETTUCE WRAPS WITH CHICKEN AND MANGO

Made for: Lunch | Prep Time: 10 minutes | Total time: 20 minutes | Servings: 4-6 people

Ingredients

- 1 lb ground chicken
- 1 mango (diced)
- 1/4 cup green onions (chopped),
- 2 tbsp soy sauce
- 1 tbsp rice vinegar
- 1 tbsp sesame oil
- 1 head of lettuce (leaves separated)

Instructions

1. In a pan, cook ground chicken over medium heat until browned.
2. Mix diced mango, green onions, soy sauce, rice vinegar, and sesame oil in a small bowl.
3. Add the mango mixture to the pan with the chicken and stir until heated.
4. Serve the chicken mixture in lettuce leaves.

Notes: You can use any lettuce leaves, like butter lettuce, romaine, or bib lettuce, for this recipe.

SPINACH AND FETA STUFFED CHICKEN

Made for: Lunch | Prep Time: 10 minutes | Total time: 30 minutes | Servings: 04 people

Ingredients

- 4 boneless
- skinless chicken breasts
- 2 cups spinach (chopped)
- 1/4 cup crumbled feta cheese
- 1/4 cup diced red bell pepper
- 1 tbsp olive oil
- 1 tsp garlic powder, salt and pepper to taste

Instructions

1. Preheat oven to 375 degrees F.
2. In a pan, sauté spinach, red bell pepper, garlic powder, and olive oil until spinach is wilted.
3. Remove from heat and stir in feta cheese.
4. Please make a small cut in the center of each chicken breast and stuff it with a spinach mixture.
5. Place chicken in a baking dish and season with salt and pepper.
6. Bake for 25-30 minutes or until chicken is cooked through.

Notes: You can use other types of cheese, like goat cheese or ricotta, for this recipe.

GRILLED PORTOBELLO MUSHROOM BURGERS

Made for: Lunch | Prep Time: 10 minutes | Total time: 20 minutes | Servings: 04 people

Ingredients

- 4 portobello mushroom caps
- 1/4 cup balsamic vinegar
- 2 tbsp olive oil
- 2 cloves garlic (minced)
- salt and pepper to taste
- 4 buns or lettuce leaves

Instructions

1. Whisk together balsamic vinegar, olive oil, garlic, salt, and pepper in a small bowl.
2. Brush mushroom caps with the marinade and grill for 5-7 minutes per side or until tender.
3. Serve mushroom caps on buns or lettuce leaves as desired.

Notes: Add toppings like lettuce, tomato, and onion to the burger for added flavor.

ZUCCHINI NOODLE PASTA

Made for: Lunch | Prep Time: 5 minutes | Total time: 15 minutes | Servings: 04 people

Ingredients

- 2 zucchinis,
- 1/4 cup olive oil,
- 2 cloves garlic (minced),
- 1/4 cup grated Parmesan cheese,
- salt and pepper to taste,
- 1/4 cup chopped basil (optional)

Instructions

1. Using a spiralizer, spiralize the zucchini into noodles.
2. In a pan, heat olive oil over medium heat and sauté garlic until fragrant.
3. Add zucchini noodles and sauté for 2-3 minutes or until tender.
4. Stir in Parmesan cheese and remove from heat.
5. Season with salt and pepper to taste.
6. Garnish with chopped basil (optional).

Notes: You can add a protein like chicken or shrimp to the pasta.

CUCUMBER AND AVOCADO SUSHI ROLLS

Made for: Lunch | Prep Time: 20 minutes | Total time: 30 minutes | Servings: 04 people

Ingredients

- 4 sheets of sushi nori
- 2 cups cooked sushi rice
- 1 cucumber (julienned)
- 1 avocado (sliced)
- 4 tbsp rice vinegar
- 2 tsp sugar
- 1 tsp salt, soy sauce, and wasabi for serving

Instructions

1. In a small saucepan, combine rice vinegar, sugar, and salt and heat until sugar is dissolved.
2. Pour the mixture over the cooked sushi rice and stir to combine.
3. Place a sheet of sushi nori, shiny side down, on a sushi rolling mat.
4. Spread a thin layer of sushi rice on the nori, leaving a 1/2-inch border at the top.
5. Arrange cucumber and avocado slices on the rice.
6. Roll the sushi using the mat, and seal the edge with water.
7. Repeat with the remaining nori sheets and filling.
8. Cut the sushi rolls into bite-sized pieces and serve with soy sauce and wasabi.

Notes: You can add other low FODMAP fillings like Tofu or bell peppers.

COCONUT CURRY SOUP

Made for: Lunch | Prep Time: 10 minutes | Total time: 30 minutes | Servings: 04 people

Ingredients

- 1 tbsp coconut oil,
- 2 cloves garlic (minced),
- 1 onion (diced),
- 1 tbsp curry powder,
- 1 can coconut milk,
- 2 cups chicken or vegetable broth,
- 1 cup diced carrots,
- 1 cup diced potatoes,
- 1 cup diced bell peppers, salt, and pepper to taste, cilantro for garnish

Instructions

1. In a pot, heat coconut oil over medium heat and sauté garlic and onion until softened.
2. Stir in curry powder and cook for 1-2 minutes.
3. Add coconut milk, chicken or vegetable broth, carrots, potatoes, and bell peppers.
4. Bring to a boil, then reduce heat and simmer for 20 minutes or until vegetables are tender.
5. Season with salt and pepper to taste.
6. Garnish with cilantro before serving.

Notes: You can add a protein like chicken or shrimp to the soup.

GARLIC AND LEMON SHRIMP SKEWERS

Made for: Lunch | Prep Time: 10 minutes | Total time: 20 minutes | Servings: 04 people

Ingredients

- 1 lb shrimp, peeled and deveined,
- 2 cloves garlic (minced),
- 2 tbsp lemon juice,
- 2 tbsp olive oil,
- salt and pepper to taste,
- skewers (soaked in water for 30 minutes)

Instructions

1. Mix garlic, lemon juice, olive oil, salt, and pepper in a small bowl.
2. Thread shrimp onto skewers and brush with the marinade.
3. Grill skewers for 2-3 minutes per side or until shrimp are pink and cooked through.
4. Serve hot.

Notes: Add vegetables like bell peppers or zucchini to the skewers for added flavor.

TUNA SALAD LETTUCE WRAPS

Made for: Lunch | Prep Time: 10 minutes | Total time: 10 minutes | Servings: 01 people

Ingredients

- 1 can of tuna, drained,
- 2 tbsp mayonnaise,
- 1 tbsp Dijon mustard,
- 1/4 cup diced celery,
- 1/4 cup diced red onion,
- salt and pepper to taste,
- lettuce leaves

Instructions

1. Mix tuna, mayonnaise, Dijon mustard, celery, and red onion in a small bowl.
2. Season with salt and pepper to taste.
3. Serve the tuna mixture in lettuce leaves.

Notes:

For added flavor, you can add other low-FODMAP ingredients like chopped pickles or capers.

STUFFED BELL PEPPERS

Made for: Lunch | Prep Time: 10 minutes | Total time: 30 minutes | Servings: 04 people

Ingredients

- 4 bell peppers (halved and seeded),
- 1 lb ground beef,
- 1/4 cup diced onion,
- 1/4 cup chopped mushrooms,
- 1/4 cup cooked rice,
- 1/4 cup grated cheese,
- 1 tsp Italian seasoning,
- salt and pepper to taste

Instructions

1. Preheat oven to 375 degrees F.
2. In a pan, brown ground beef and add onion and mushrooms; cook until softened.
3. Stir in cooked rice, grated cheese, Italian seasoning, salt, and pepper.
4. Stuff the mixture into the bell pepper halves and place in a baking dish.
5. Bake for 25-30 minutes or until bell peppers is tender.

Notes: You can use ground meat like turkey or pork and cheese like cheddar or mozzarella.

ROASTED EGGPLANT AND TOMATO PASTA

Made for: Lunch | Prep Time: 10 minutes | Total time: 40 minutes | Servings: 04 people

Ingredients

- 1 eggplant, diced,
- 2 cups cherry tomatoes, halved,
- 1/4 cup olive oil,
- 2 cloves garlic (minced),
- 1/4 cup chopped basil,
- 8 oz pasta of your choice,
- salt and pepper to taste

Instructions

1. Preheat oven to 400 degrees F.
2. On a baking sheet, toss eggplant and tomatoes with olive oil, garlic, salt, and pepper.
3. Roast for 20-25 minutes or until eggplant and tomatoes are tender.
4. Cook pasta according to package instructions and toss with the roasted vegetables.
5. Garnish with chopped basil.

Notes:

You can use other types of vegetables like zucchini or bell peppers in this recipe.

PESTO AND TOMATO GRILLED CHEESE SANDWICH

Made for: Lunch | Prep Time: 5 minutes | Total time: 15 minutes | Servings: 02 people

Ingredients

- 4 slices of
- bread of your choice,
- 2 tbsp basil pesto,
- 1/4 cup diced tomatoes,
- 1/4 cup grated cheese,
- 1 tbsp butter

Instructions

1. Spread pesto on two slices of bread.
2. Top with diced tomatoes and grated cheese.
3. Close the sandwich with the remaining slices of bread.
4. Melt butter in a pan over medium heat.
5. Place the sandwich in the pan and grill for 2-3 minutes per side until the bread is golden brown and the cheese is melted.
6. Cut in half and serve warm.

Notes:

This recipe can use other cheese types like mozzarella or cheddar.

GREEN SALAD WITH LEMON VINAIGRETTE

Made for: Lunch | Prep Time: 5 minutes | Total time: 5 minutes | Servings: 04 people

Ingredients

- 4 cups mixed greens
- 1/4 cup diced cucumber
- 1/4 cup chopped bell pepper
- 1/4 cup diced red onion
- 2 tbsp olive oil
- 1 tbsp lemon juice
- 1 tsp honey
- salt and pepper to taste

Instructions

1. Mix mixed greens, cucumber, bell pepper, and red onion in a large bowl.
2. Whisk together olive oil, lemon juice, honey, salt, and pepper in a small bowl.
3. Pour the vinaigrette over the salad and toss to combine.
4. Serve chilled.

Notes:

For added flavor, you can add other low-FODMAP fruits or vegetables like strawberries or avocado.

SESAME TOFU STIR FRY

Made for: Lunch | Prep Time: 10 minutes | Total time: 20 minutes | Servings: 04 people

Ingredients

- 1 lb firm tofu, diced,
- 2 tbsp sesame oil,
- 2 cloves garlic (minced),
- 1/4 cup chopped bell peppers,
- 1/4 cup diced carrots,
- 2 tbsp soy sauce,
- 1 tbsp rice vinegar,
- 1 tsp sesame seeds

Instructions

1. Press the tofu to remove any excess water and cut it into cubes.
2. Heat sesame oil over medium heat and sauté garlic until fragrant.
3. Add bell peppers, carrots, tofu, soy sauce, and vinegar.
4. Cook for 5-7 minutes or until vegetables is tender.
5. Sprinkle with sesame seeds before serving.

Notes:

For added flavor, you can add other low-FODMAP vegetables like broccoli or bok choy.

COBB SALAD WITH GRILLED CHICKEN

Made for: Lunch | Prep Time: 10 minutes | Total time: 25 minutes | Servings: 04 people

Ingredients

- 2 boneless, skinless chicken breasts,
- 4 cups mixed greens,
- 1/4 cup diced tomatoes,
- 1/4 cup diced cucumber,
- 1/4 cup diced red onion,
- 1/4 cup crumbled bacon,
- 2 tbsp olive oil,
- 1 tbsp red wine vinegar,
- salt and pepper to taste

Instructions

1. Grill chicken over medium heat for 6-8 minutes per side or until cooked.
2. Mix mixed greens, tomatoes, cucumber, red onion, and crumbled bacon in a large bowl.
3. Whisk together olive oil, red wine vinegar, salt, and pepper in a small bowl.
4. Pour the dressing over the salad and toss to combine.
5. Slice the chicken and add it to the salad.
6. Serve chilled.

Notes:

For added flavor, you can add other low FODMAP ingredients like chopped hard-boiled eggs or avocado.

SPICY BLACK BEAN AND SWEET POTATO TACOS

Made for: Lunch | Prep Time: 10 minutes | Total time: 30 minutes | Servings: 04 people

Ingredients

- 1 sweet potato, diced,
- 1 can black beans (rinsed and drained),
- 1/4 cup diced red onion,
- 1/4 cup diced bell pepper,
- 1 tbsp chili powder,
- 1 tsp cumin,
- 1/4 cup chopped cilantro,
- 8 corn tortillas,
- sour cream and lime wedges for serving

Instructions

1. Preheat oven to 375 degrees F.
2. Toss sweet potato with olive oil, chili powder, and cumin on a baking sheet.
3. Roast for 25-30 minutes or until tender.
4. In a pan, sauté red onion and bell pepper until softened.
5. Add black beans and cooked sweet potato, and heat through.
6. Stir in cilantro.
7. Serve the mixture in corn tortillas and serve with sour cream and lime wedges.

Notes:

You can also add other low FODMAP toppings like shredded cheese or guacamole.

LEMON AND HERB GRILLED CHICKEN

Made for: Lunch | Prep Time: 10 minutes | Total time: 25 minutes | Servings: 04 people

Ingredients

- 4 boneless,
- skinless chicken breasts,
- 2 tbsp olive oil,
- 2 cloves garlic (minced),
- 1 tbsp lemon juice,
- 1 tsp dried thyme,
- 1 tsp dried rosemary,
- salt and pepper to taste

Instructions

1. Mix olive oil, garlic, lemon juice, thyme, rosemary, salt, and pepper in a small bowl.
2. Brush chicken with the marinade and grill over medium heat for 6-8 minutes per side or until cooked.
3. Serve hot.

Notes:

For added flavor, you can add other low-FODMAP herbs like parsley or basil to the marinade.

CREAMY TOMATO AND BASIL SOUP

Made for: Lunch | Prep Time: 10 minutes | Total time: 30 minutes | Servings: 04 people

Ingredients

- 1 tbsp olive oil,
- 2 cloves garlic (minced),
- 1 onion (diced),
- 28 oz can of diced tomatoes,
- 2 cups chicken or vegetable broth,
- 1/4 cup heavy cream,
- 1/4 cup chopped basil,
- salt and pepper to taste

Instructions

1. In a pot, heat olive oil over medium heat and sauté garlic and onion until softened.
2. Stir in diced tomatoes and chicken or vegetable broth.
3. Bring to a boil, then reduce heat and simmer for 20 minutes.
4. Stir in heavy cream and chopped basil.
5. Season with salt and pepper to taste.
6. Serve hot.

Notes:

You can also add other low-FODMAP vegetables like bell peppers or zucchini to the soup.

PORK AND APPLE SKEWERS

Made for: Lunch | Prep Time: 10 minutes | Total time: 25 minutes | Servings: 04 people

Ingredients

- 1 lb pork tenderloin, diced
- 2 tbsp olive oil
- 2 cloves garlic (minced)
- 1 tsp dried thyme
- 1 tsp dried rosemary
- salt and pepper to taste
- skewers (soaked in water for 30 minutes),
- 1 apple (cored and diced)

Instructions

1. Mix olive oil, garlic, thyme, rosemary, salt, and pepper in a small bowl.
2. Thread pork and apple onto skewers and brush with the marinade.
3. Grill skewers for 8-10 minutes per side or until pork is cooked through.
4. Serve hot.

Notes:

For added flavor, you can add other low-FODMAP vegetables like bell peppers or zucchini to the skewers.

SPINACH AND FETA STUFFED CHICKEN BREASTS

Made for: Lunch | Prep Time: 10 minutes | Total time: 40 minutes | Servings: 04 people

Ingredients

- 4 boneless,
- skinless chicken breasts,
- 1/2 cup crumbled feta cheese,
- 1/2 cup cooked spinach,
- 2 cloves garlic (minced),
- 1/4 cup diced red onion,
- 1 tsp dried oregano,
- salt and pepper to taste,
- 2 tbsp olive oil

Instructions

1. Preheat oven to 375 degrees F.
2. Mix feta cheese, spinach, garlic, red onion, oregano, salt, and pepper in a small bowl.
3. Cut a pocket into the side of each chicken breast and stuff it with the feta mixture.
4. Brush chicken with olive oil and season with salt and pepper.
5. Place chicken in a baking dish and bake for 30-35 minutes or until cooked.
6. Serve hot.

Notes: You can add other low FODMAP herbs like thyme or rosemary to the stuffing for added flavor.

LEMON AND HERB QUINOA SALAD

Made for: Lunch | Prep Time: 10 minutes | Total time: 30 minutes | Servings: 04 people

Ingredients

- 1 cup quinoa,
- cooked and cooled,
- 1/4 cup diced bell pepper,
- 1/4 cup diced cucumber,
- 1/4 cup diced red onion,
- 2 tbsp lemon juice,
- 2 tbsp olive oil,
- 1 tsp dried thyme,
- 1 tsp dried rosemary,
- salt and pepper to taste

Instructions

1. Combine quinoa, bell pepper, cucumber, and red onion in a large bowl.
2. Whisk together lemon juice, olive oil, thyme, rosemary, salt, and pepper in a small bowl.
3. Pour the dressing over the quinoa mixture and toss to combine.
4. Serve chilled.

Notes:

For added flavor, you can add other low FODMAP ingredients like chopped cherry tomatoes or avocado.

CAULIFLOWER FRIED RICE

Made for: Lunch | Prep Time: 10 minutes | Total time: 30 minutes | Servings: 04 people

Ingredients

- 1 head of cauliflower, grated,
- 2 tbsp sesame oil,
- 2 cloves garlic (minced),
- 1/4 cup diced onion,
- 1/4 cup diced carrots,
- 1/4 cup peas,
- 2 tbsp soy sauce,
- 1 tbsp rice vinegar,
- 1 tsp sesame seeds

Instructions

1. Heat sesame oil over medium heat and sauté garlic, onion, carrots, and peas until softened.
2. Stir in grated cauliflower, soy sauce, and rice vinegar.
3. Cook for 5-7 minutes or until cauliflower is tender.
4. Sprinkle with sesame seeds before serving.

Notes:

For added flavor, you can add other low-FODMAP vegetables like bell peppers or bok choy.

LENTIL AND VEGETABLE STEW

Made for: Lunch | Prep Time: 10 minutes | Total time: 30 minutes | Servings: 04 people

Ingredients

- 1 tbsp olive oil,
- 2 cloves garlic (minced),
- 1 onion (diced),
- 1 cup diced carrots,
- 1 cup diced potatoes,
- 1 cup green lentils,
- 4 cups vegetable broth,
- 1 tsp dried thyme,
- 1 tsp dried rosemary,
- salt and pepper to taste

Instructions

1. In a pot, heat olive oil over medium heat and sauté garlic and onion until softened.
2. Add carrots, potatoes, lentils, vegetable broth, thyme, rosemary, salt, and pepper.
3. Bring to a boil, then reduce heat and simmer for 20-25 minutes or until vegetables and lentils are tender.
4. Serve hot.

Notes:

You can add other low-FODMAP vegetables like bell peppers or zucchini to the stew.

BEEF AND BROCCOLI STIR FRY

Made for: Lunch | Prep Time: 10 minutes | Total time: 20 minutes | Servings: 04 people

Ingredients

- 1 lb flank steak, thinly sliced,
- 2 tbsp vegetable oil,
- 2 cloves garlic (minced),
- 1 head of broccoli, cut into florets,
- 2 tbsp soy sauce,
- 1 tbsp rice vinegar,
- 1 tsp cornstarch

Instructions

1. Mix soy sauce, rice vinegar, and cornstarch in a small bowl.
2. Heat vegetable oil over medium heat and sauté garlic until fragrant.
3. Add beef and cook for 2-3 minutes per side or until browned.
4. Add broccoli and stir-fry for 3-5 minutes or until tender.
5. Pour the soy sauce mixture over the beef and broccoli, and stir until thickened.
6. Serve hot.

Notes:

For added flavor, you can add other low-FODMAP vegetables like bell peppers or bok choy.

CREAMY GARLIC AND MUSHROOM CHICKEN

Made for: Lunch | Prep Time: 10 minutes | Total time: 30 minutes | Servings: 04 people

Ingredients

- 4 boneless,
- skinless chicken breasts,
- 1/4 cup diced onion,
- 1/4 cup sliced mushrooms,
- 2 cloves garlic (minced),
- 1/4 cup heavy cream,
- 1 tbsp flour,
- 1 tsp dried thyme,
- salt and pepper to taste,
- 2 tbsp olive oil

Instructions

1. In a pan, heat olive oil and sauté onion, mushrooms, and garlic until softened.
2. Mix heavy cream, flour, thyme, salt, and pepper in a small bowl.
3. Add the cream mixture to the pan and stir until thickened.
4. Add chicken and cook for 8-10 minutes per side or until cooked through.
5. Serve hot.

Notes:

You can also add other low FODMAP vegetables like bell peppers or zucchini to the dish for added flavor.

STUFFED ZUCCHINI BOATS

Made for: Lunch | Prep Time: 10 minutes | Total time: 30 minutes | Servings: 04 people

Ingredients

- 4 zucchinis, halved and seeded,
- 1 lb ground beef,
- 1/4 cup diced onion,
- 1/4 cup chopped mushrooms,
- 1/4 cup cooked rice,
- 1/4 cup grated cheese,
- 1 tsp Italian seasoning,
- salt and pepper to taste

Instructions

1. Preheat oven to 375 degrees F.
2. In a pan, brown ground beef and add onion and mushrooms; cook until softened.
3. Stir in cooked rice, grated cheese, Italian seasoning, salt, and pepper.
4. Fill the zucchini halves with the beef mixture and place them in a baking dish.
5. Bake for 25-30 minutes or until zucchinis are tender.
6. Serve hot.

Notes:

You can add other low FODMAP vegetables like bell peppers or spinach to the filling for added flavor.

TUNA SALAD LETTUCE WRAPS

Made for: Lunch | Prep Time: 10 minutes | Total time: 10 minutes | Servings: 04 people

Ingredients

- 2 cans of tuna, drained and flaked,
- 1/4 cup diced celery,
- 1/4 cup diced red onion,
- 2 tbsp mayonnaise,
- 2 tsp Dijon mustard,
- 1 tsp lemon juice,
- salt and pepper to taste,
- 8 lettuce leaves

Instructions

1. Mix tuna, celery, red onion, mayonnaise, Dijon mustard, lemon juice, salt, and pepper in a bowl.
2. Spoon mixture onto lettuce leaves and wrap up.
3. Serve chilled.

Notes:

You can also add other low FODMAP ingredients like diced apples or grapes to the tuna salad for added flavor.

GRILLED EGGPLANT AND MOZZARELLA SANDWICHES

Made for: Lunch | Prep Time: 10 minutes | Total time: 20 minutes | Servings: 04 people

Ingredients

- 2 eggplants, sliced,
- 2 tbsp olive oil,
- 2 cloves garlic (minced),
- 1/4 cup diced tomatoes,
- 1/4 cup fresh mozzarella cheese,
- 1 tbsp balsamic vinegar,
- salt and pepper to taste,
- 4 slices of bread of your choice

Instructions

1. Mix olive oil, garlic, salt, and pepper in a small bowl.
2. Brush eggplant slices with the mixture and grill over medium heat for 3-4 minutes per side or until tender.
3. Mix diced tomatoes, balsamic vinegar, and salt and pepper in a small bowl.
4. Assemble sandwiches with eggplant, tomato mixture, and mozzarella cheese.
5. Grill sandwiches for 2-3 minutes per side or until bread is golden brown and cheese is melted.
6. Cut in half and serve warm.

Notes:

For added flavor, you can add other low-FODMAP ingredients like pesto or basil leaves.

SPINACH AND RICOTTA STUFFED SHELLS

Made for: Lunch | Prep Time: 10 minutes | Total time: 30 minutes | Servings: 04 people

Ingredients

- 12 jumbo pasta shells,
- 1/2 cup ricotta cheese,
- 1/2 cup cooked spinach,
- 1/4 cup grated Parmesan cheese,
- 1/4 cup diced onion,
- 1 clove garlic (minced),
- 1 tsp dried basil,
- salt and pepper to taste,
- 1 cup marinara sauce

Instructions

1. Preheat oven to 375 degrees F.
2. Cook pasta shells according to package instructions, drain, and set aside.
3. Mix ricotta cheese, spinach, Parmesan cheese, onion, garlic, basil, salt, and pepper in a small bowl.
4. Stuff the shells with the ricotta mixture and place them in a baking dish.
5. Pour marinara sauce over the shells.
6. Bake for 25-30 minutes or until heated through.
7. Serve hot.

Notes: You can add other low FODMAP vegetables like diced bell peppers or mushrooms to the filling for added flavor.

PESTO CHICKEN AND VEGETABLE SKEWERS

Made for: Lunch | Prep Time: 10 minutes | Total time: 30 minutes | Servings: 04 people

Ingredients

- 1 lb boneless,
- skinless chicken breasts, diced,
- 1/4 cup chopped bell peppers,
- 1/4 cup diced zucchini,
- 1/4 cup chopped onion,
- 2 tbsp basil pesto,
- salt and pepper to taste,
- skewers (soaked in water for 30 minutes)

Instructions

1. Preheat the grill to medium-high heat.
2. Thread chicken, bell peppers, zucchini, and onion onto skewers.
3. Brush skewers with pesto and season with salt and pepper.
4. Grill skewers for 8-10 minutes per side or until chicken is cooked through.
5. Serve hot.

Notes:

You can add other low FODMAP vegetables like mushrooms or cherry tomatoes to the skewers for added flavor.

Low Fodmap Dinner

Welcome to our collection of delicious and mouthwatering low-FODMAP dinner recipes! These recipes are perfect for individuals following a low FODMAP diet to manage symptoms related to conditions such as Irritable Bowel Syndrome (IBS).

Our collection of recipes includes a wide variety of options sure to please even the pickiest of eaters. From hearty stews and soups to flavorful stir-fries and grilled dishes, there is something for everyone to enjoy. Not only are these recipes delicious, but they are also easy to prepare and can be on the table in 30 minutes or less.

In addition to relieving IBS symptoms, following a low FODMAP diet can also improve overall gut health and digestion. By eliminating certain high FODMAP foods, you may notice an improvement in symptoms such as constipation, diarrhea, and abdominal pain.

So, whether you are new to the low FODMAP diet or looking for fresh and delicious dinner options, our collection of recipes is sure to inspire and delight you. So, let's get cooking!

CREAMY CHICKEN AND MUSHROOM PASTA

Made for: Dinner | Prep Time: 10 minutes | Total time: 2 5 | Servings: Grated Parmesan cheese

Ingredients

- 8 oz of boneless chicken breast, cut into bite-size pieces
- 8 oz of sliced mushrooms
- 1 cup of heavy cream
- 2 cloves of garlic, minced
- 2 tablespoons of butter
- Salt and pepper, to taste
- 8 oz of your favorite pasta

Instructions

1. Cook pasta according to package instructions until al dente. Drain and set aside.
2. In a large skillet, melt the butter over medium-high heat. Add the chicken and cook for about 5 minutes or until browned.
3. Add the mushrooms and garlic and cook for another 5 minutes.
4. Pour in the heavy cream and bring to a simmer. Season with salt and pepper, to taste.
5. Add the cooked pasta to the skillet and toss to coat with the sauce.
6. Serve with grated Parmesan cheese on top.

GRILLED SALMON WITH LEMON AND HERB

Made for: Dinner | Prep Time: 10 minutes | Total time: 2 0 | Servings: Fresh lemon wedges

Fresh herbs, chopped

Ingredients

- 4 6-oz salmon fillets
- 2 tablespoons of olive oil
- 1 teaspoon of dried thyme
- 1 teaspoon of dried basil
- 1 teaspoon of dried parsley
- 1/2 teaspoon of salt
- 1/4 teaspoon of black pepper
- 1/4 cup of lemon juice

Instructions

1. Preheat grill to medium-high heat.
2. In a small bowl, mix together the olive oil, thyme, basil, parsley, salt, and pepper.
3. Brush the salmon fillets with the herb mixture, then place them on the grill.
4. Grill for about 6-8 minutes per side, or until the salmon is cooked through.
5. Remove from the grill and brush with lemon juice.

Serve with fresh lemon wedges and chopped herbs

SLOW COOKER BEEF STEW

Made for: Dinner | Prep Time: 15 minutes | Total time: 8 hours | Servings: Fresh parsley, chopped

Ingredients

- 2 lbs of beef chuck, cut into bite-size pieces
- 2 cups of beef broth
- 1 cup of red wine
- 1 cup of diced carrots
- 1 cup of diced potatoes
- 1 cup of diced onion
- 2 cloves of garlic, minced
- 1 teaspoon of dried thyme
- 1 teaspoon of dried rosemary
- Salt and pepper, to taste

Instructions

1. Add all ingredients to a slow cooker and stir to combine.
2. Cover and cook on low for 8 hours, or until the beef is tender.
3. Season with salt and pepper, to taste.
4. Serve with chopped parsley on top.

SPINACH AND FETA STUFFED PORK TENDERLOIN

Made for: Dinner | Prep Time: 15 minutes | Total time: 45 | Servings: Lemon wedges

Ingredients

- 1 lb of pork tenderloin
- 1 cup of fresh spinach, chopped
- 1/2 cup of crumbled feta cheese
- 2 cloves of garlic, minced
- 1 teaspoon of dried oregano
- Salt and pepper, to taste
- 2 tablespoons of olive oil

Instructions

1. Preheat oven to 375°F.
2. Cut a pocket in the pork tenderloin by slicing it horizontally, being careful not to cut all the way through.
3. In a small bowl, mix together the spinach, feta cheese, garlic, oregano, salt, and pepper.
4. Stuff the spinach mixture into the pocket of the pork tenderloin.
5. Heat the olive oil in a large skillet over medium-high heat. Add the pork and brown on all sides.
6. Transfer the pork to a baking dish and bake in the preheated oven for 20-25 minutes or until the internal temperature reaches 145°F.
7. Let rest for 5 minutes before slicing.
8. Serve with lemon wedges on the side.

SHRIMP AND BROCCOLI STIR FRY

Made for: Dinner | Prep Time: 15 minutes | Total time: 2 0 | Servings: cooked rice

Ingredients

- 1 lb of raw shrimp, peeled and deveined
- 2 cups of broccoli florets
- 2 cloves of garlic, minced
- 2 tablespoons of soy sauce
- 2 tablespoons of rice vinegar
- 1 tablespoon of cornstarch
- 1 teaspoon of sesame oil
- 1 teaspoon of sugar
- Salt and pepper, to taste
- 2 tablespoons of vegetable oil

Instructions

1. In a small bowl, mix together the soy sauce, rice vinegar, cornstarch, sesame oil, and sugar.
2. Heat the vegetable oil in a large skillet or wok over high heat.
3. Add the shrimp and stir-fry for 2-3 minutes or until pink and cooked through.
4. Remove from skillet and set aside.
5. Add the broccoli and garlic to the skillet and stir-fry for 2-3 minutes or until tender-crisp.
6. Add the sauce and shrimp to the skillet and stir-fry for another 1-2 minutes, or until the sauce is thickened and the shrimp is heated through.
7. Season with salt and pepper, to taste.

CREAMY TOMATO AND BASIL SOUP

Made for: Dinner | Prep Time: 10 minutes | Total time: 25 | Servings: Grated Parmesan cheese Croutons

Ingredients

- 2 cups of crushed tomatoes
- 1 cup of heavy cream
- 1 cup of chicken or vegetable broth
- 1/4 cup of chopped fresh basil
- 2 cloves of garlic, minced
- 2 tablespoons of olive oil
- Salt and pepper, to taste

Instructions

1. Heat the olive oil in a large pot over medium heat. Add the garlic and cook for 1-2 minutes.
2. Add the crushed tomatoes, cream, broth, basil, salt, and pepper. Bring to a simmer and cook for 10-15 minutes.
3. Use an immersion blender to blend the soup until smooth.

Serve with grated Parmesan cheese and croutons on top.

LEMON AND HERB ROASTED CHICKEN

Made for: Dinner | Prep Time: 10 minutes | Total time: 1 hour | Servings: Fresh lemon wedges, Fresh herbs, chopped

Ingredients

- 1 whole chicken
- 2 lemons, zested and juiced
- 2 cloves of garlic, minced
- 2 tablespoons of olive oil
- 1 teaspoon of dried thyme
- 1 teaspoon of dried rosemary
- Salt and pepper, to taste

Instructions

1. Preheat oven to 425°F.
2. In a small bowl, mix together the lemon zest, lemon juice, garlic, olive oil, thyme, rosemary, salt, and pepper.
3. Place the chicken in a roasting pan and brush the lemon and herb mixture all over the chicken.
4. Roast in the preheated oven for 45-60 minutes, or until the internal temperature reaches 165°F.
5. Let rest for 10 minutes before slicing.

Serve with fresh lemon wedges and chopped herbs on top.

CRISPY BAKED CHICKEN TENDERS

Made for: Dinner | *Prep Time: 10 minutes* | *Total time: 25* | *Servings: Ranch dressing*

Ingredients

- 1 lb of chicken tenders
- 1 cup of panko bread crumbs
- 1/2 cup of grated Parmesan cheese
- 1 teaspoon of dried basil
- 1 teaspoon of dried oregano
- Salt and pepper, to taste
- 2 eggs, beaten
- 2 tablespoons of olive oil

Instructions

1. Preheat oven to 425°F.
2. In a shallow dish, mix together the panko bread crumbs, Parmesan cheese, basil, oregano, salt, and pepper.
3. Dip the chicken tenders in the beaten eggs, then coat in the panko mixture.
4. Place the chicken tenders on a baking sheet lined with parchment paper and drizzle with olive oil.
5. Bake in the preheated oven for 15-20 minutes or until golden brown and crispy.
6. Serve with ranch dressing on the side.

SLOW COOKER BBQ PULLED PORK

Made for: Dinner | Prep Time: 15 minutes | Total time: 8 hours | Servings: Buns

Ingredients

- 2 lbs of pork shoulder
- 1 cup of BBQ sauce
- 1/2 cup of chicken broth
- 1/4 cup of apple cider vinegar
- 2 cloves of garlic, minced
- 1 teaspoon of smoked paprika
- 1 teaspoon of dried thyme
- Salt and pepper, to taste

Instructions

1. Add all ingredients to a slow cooker and stir to combine.
2. Cover and cook on low for 8 hours, or until the pork is tender and shreds easily.
3. Shred the pork with two forks.
4. Serve on buns.

SPAGHETTI BOLOGNESE

Made for: Dinner *| Prep Time: 15 minutes | Total time: 45 | Servings: Grated Parmesan cheese*

Ingredients

- 1 lb of ground beef
- 1 cup of diced onion
- 1 cup of diced carrot
- 1 cup of diced celery
- 2 cloves of garlic, minced
- 1 can of diced tomatoes
- 1 cup of red wine
- 2 tablespoons of tomato paste
- 1 teaspoon of dried oregano
- Salt and pepper, to taste
- 8 oz of spaghetti

Instructions

1. Cook the spaghetti according to package instructions until al dente. Drain and set aside.
2. In a large skillet, brown the ground beef over medium-high heat. Drain any excess fat.
3. Add the onion, carrot, celery, and garlic and cook for another 5 minutes.
4. Pour in the diced tomatoes, red wine, tomato paste, oregano, salt, and pepper. Bring to a simmer and cook for 20-25 minutes or until the vegetables are tender and the sauce has thickened.
5. Toss the cooked spaghetti with the bolognese sauce.
6. Serve with grated Parmesan cheese on top.

GARLIC AND HERB GRILLED VEGETABLES

Made for: Dinner | Prep Time: 10 minutes | Total time: 15 | Servings: Lemon wedges

Ingredients

- 1 cup of sliced bell peppers
- 1 cup of sliced zucchini
- 1 cup of sliced onion
- 2 cloves of garlic, minced
- 2 tablespoons of olive oil
- 1 teaspoon of dried thyme
- 1 teaspoon of dried basil
- Salt and pepper, to taste

Instructions

1. Preheat grill to medium-high heat.
2. In a small bowl, mix together the olive oil, garlic, thyme, basil, salt, and pepper.
3. Brush the vegetables with the herb mixture and place them on the grill.
4. Grill for about 5-7 minutes per side, or until tender and charred.
5. Serve with lemon wedges on the side.

POTATO AND LEEK SOUP

Made for: Dinner | Prep Time: 10 minutes | Total time: 30 | Servings: Croutons, Grated Parmesan cheese

Ingredients

- 2 cups of diced potatoes
- 1 cup of sliced leeks, white and light green parts only
- 2 cloves of garlic, minced
- 2 cups of chicken or vegetable broth
- 1 cup of heavy cream
- 2 tablespoons of butter
- Salt and pepper, to taste

Instructions

1. Melt the butter in a large pot over medium heat. Add the leeks and garlic and cook for 2-3 minutes.
2. Add the potatoes, broth, and cream. Bring to a simmer and cook for 15-20 minutes or until the potatoes are tender.
3. Use an immersion blender to blend the soup until smooth.
4. Season with salt and pepper, to taste.
5. Serve with croutons and grated Parmesan cheese on top.

BAKED EGGPLANT PARMESAN

Made for: Dinner | *Prep Time: 20 minutes* | *Total time: 1 hour* | *Servings: Fresh basil, chopped*

Ingredients

- 2 medium eggplants, sliced
- 1 cup of all-purpose flour
- 2 eggs, beaten
- 2 cups of breadcrumbs
- 1 cup of grated mozzarella cheese
- 1 cup of grated Parmesan cheese
- 1 cup of marinara sauce
- Salt and pepper, to taste
- Olive oil, for brushing

Instructions

1. Preheat oven to 375°F.
2. Season the eggplant slices with salt and pepper.
3. Place the flour in one shallow dish, the beaten eggs in another, and the breadcrumbs in a third.
4. Dip the eggplant slices in the flour, then the eggs, and finally the breadcrumbs.
5. Place the eggplant slices on a baking sheet lined with parchment paper and brush with olive oil.
6. Bake in the preheated oven for 20-25 minutes or until golden brown and crispy.
7. Spread a layer of marinara sauce in the bottom of a baking dish. Place a layer of eggplant slices on top, then sprinkle with mozzarella and Parmesan cheese. Repeat the layers until all the eggplant slices are used up.
8. Bake for another 20-25 minutes or until the cheese is melted and bubbly.

LEMON AND HERB GRILLED SALMON

Made for: Dinner | Prep Time: 10 minutes | Total time: 2 0 | Servings: Fresh lemon wedges, Fresh herbs, chopped

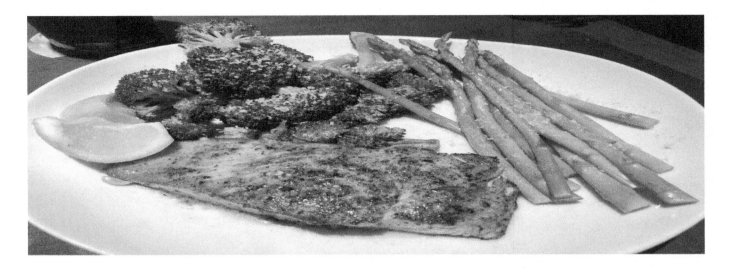

Ingredients

- 4 salmon fillets
- 2 lemons, zested and juiced
- 2 cloves of garlic, minced
- 2 tablespoons of olive oil
- 1 teaspoon of dried thyme
- 1 teaspoon of dried basil
- Salt and pepper, to taste

Instructions

1. Preheat grill to medium-high heat.
2. In a small bowl, mix together the lemon zest, lemon juice, garlic, olive oil, thyme, basil, salt, and pepper.
3. Brush the salmon fillets with the herb mixture and place them on the grill.
4. Grill for about 4-6 minutes per side, or until cooked through.
5. Serve with fresh lemon wedges and chopped herbs on top.

MEATLOAF

Made for: Dinner | Prep Time: 10 minutes | Total time: 1 hour | Servings: Mashed potatoes

Ingredients

- 1 lb of ground beef
- 1/2 cup of breadcrumbs
- 1/4 cup of grated onion
- 1 egg, beaten
- 2 cloves of garlic, minced
- 1/4 cup of ketchup
- 2 tablespoons of Worcestershire sauce
- Salt and pepper, to taste

Instructions

1. Preheat oven to 375°F.
2. In a large bowl, mix together the ground beef, breadcrumbs, onion, egg, garlic, ketchup, Worcestershire sauce, salt, and pepper.
3. Shape the mixture into a loaf and place it in a baking dish.
4. Bake in the preheated oven for 45-50 minutes or until the internal temperature reaches 165°F.
5. Let rest for 10 minutes before slicing.
6. Serve with mashed potatoes on the side.

BLACK BEAN AND SWEET POTATO ENCHILADAS

Made for: Dinner | Prep Time: 20 minutes | Total time: 40 | Servings: Sour cream, Chopped cilantro

Ingredients

- 2 cups of diced sweet potatoes
- 1 can of black beans, drained and rinsed
- 1 cup of diced onion
- 2 cloves of garlic, minced
- 1 cup of enchilada sauce
- 1 cup of grated cheddar cheese
- Salt and pepper, to taste
- 8 corn tortillas

Instructions

1. Preheat oven to 375°F.
2. In a large skillet, cook the sweet potatoes, onion, and garlic over medium-high heat until the sweet potatoes are tender.
3. Stir in the black beans and enchilada sauce and season with salt and pepper.
4. Place a spoonful of the sweet potato mixture onto each tortilla, roll it up, and place it in a baking dish.
5. Pour any remaining enchilada sauce over the top and sprinkle with the grated cheese.
6. Bake in the preheated oven for 15-20 minutes or until the cheese is melted and bubbly.
7. Serve with sour cream and chopped cilantro on top.

BAKED COD WITH TOMATOES AND CAPERS

Made for: Dinner *| Prep Time: 10 minutes | Total time: 2 0 | Servings: Lemon wedges, Fresh parsley, chopped*

Ingredients

- 4 cod fillets
- 2 cups of cherry tomatoes, halved
- 2 tablespoons of capers
- 2 cloves of garlic, minced
- 2 tablespoons of olive oil
- 1 tablespoon of lemon juice
- 1 teaspoon of dried oregano
- Salt and pepper, to taste

Instructions

1. Preheat oven to 425°F.
2. In a small bowl, mix together the olive oil, lemon juice, garlic, oregano, salt, and pepper.
3. Place the cod fillets in a baking dish and top with the cherry tomatoes and capers.
4. Drizzle the tomato mixture with the olive oil mixture.
5. Bake in the preheated oven for 12-15 minutes or until the fish is cooked through.
6. Serve with lemon wedges and fresh parsley on top.

PAN-SEARED SCALLOPS WITH LEMON BUTTER SAUCE

Made for: Dinner | Prep Time: 10 minutes | Total time: 2 0 | Servings: Lemon wedges, Fresh parsley, chopped

Ingredients

- 1 lb of scallops
- 2 tablespoons of butter
- 2 cloves of garlic, minced
- 1/4 cup of white wine
- 1/4 cup of chicken broth
- 1 lemon, juiced
- 1 teaspoon of dried thyme
- Salt and pepper, to taste

Instructions

1. Heat a large skillet over high heat.
2. Season the scallops with salt and pepper.
3. Add the scallops to the skillet and cook for 2-3 minutes per side or until golden brown. Remove from skillet and set aside.
4. In the same skillet, add the butter and garlic and cook until fragrant.
5. Add the white wine, chicken broth, lemon juice, thyme, salt and pepper. Cook for 2-3 minutes or until the sauce has thickened.
6. Return the scallops to the skillet and toss in the sauce.
7. Serve with lemon wedges and fresh parsley on top.

CHICKEN PARMESAN

Made for: Dinner | Prep Tim e: 10 minutes | Total time: 30 | Servings: Fresh basil, chopped

Ingredients

- 4 chicken breasts
- 1 cup of all-purpose flour
- 2 eggs, beaten
- 2 cups of breadcrumbs
- 1 cup of marinara sauce
- 1 cup of grated mozzarella cheese
- 1/4 cup of grated Parmesan cheese
- Salt and pepper, to taste
- Olive oil, for brushing

Instructions

1. Preheat oven to 375°F.
2. Season the chicken breasts with salt and pepper.
3. Place the flour in one shallow dish, the beaten eggs in another, and the breadcrumbs in a third.
4. Dip the chicken breasts in the flour, then the eggs, and finally the breadcrumbs.
5. Place the chicken breasts on a baking sheet lined with parchment paper and brush with olive oil.
6. Bake in the preheated oven for 20-25 minutes or until the chicken is cooked through and golden brown.
7. Spread a layer of marinara sauce in the bottom of a baking dish. Place the chicken on top and sprinkle with mozzarella and Parmesan cheese.
8. Bake for another 10-15 minutes or until the cheese is melted and bubbly.
9. Serve with fresh basil on top.

TURKEY AND VEGETABLE MEATBALLS

Made for: Dinner | Prep Time: 15 minutes | Total time: 30 | Servings: Cooked spaghetti, Grated Parmesan cheese

Ingredients

- 1 lb of ground turkey
- 1 cup of grated carrots
- 1/2 cup of grated zucchini
- 1/4 cup of grated onion
- 2 cloves of garlic, minced
- 1 egg, beaten
- 1/4 cup of breadcrumbs
- 1 teaspoon of dried oregano
- Salt and pepper, to taste
- 2 tablespoons of olive oil

Instructions

1. Preheat oven to 375°F.
2. In a large bowl, mix together the ground turkey, carrots, zucchini, onion, garlic, egg, breadcrumbs, oregano, salt, and pepper.
3. Form the mixture into meatballs and place them on a baking sheet lined with parchment paper.
4. Brush the meatballs with olive oil.
5. Bake in the preheated oven for 20-25 minutes or until cooked through.
6. Serve with cooked spaghetti and grated Parmesan cheese on top.

SPINACH AND FETA STUFFED CHICKEN

Made for: Dinner | Prep Time: 15 minutes | Total time: 30 | Servings: Lemon wedges, Fresh parsley, chopped

Ingredients

- 4 chicken breasts
- 1 cup of spinach, chopped
- 1/4 cup of crumbled feta cheese
- 2 cloves of garlic, minced
- 1 teaspoon of dried oregano
- Salt and pepper, to taste
- 2 tablespoons of olive oil

Instructions

1. Preheat oven to 375°F.
2. In a small bowl, mix together the spinach, feta cheese, garlic, oregano, salt, and pepper.
3. Cut a pocket in each chicken breast and stuff with the spinach mixture.
4. Brush the chicken with olive oil and season with salt and pepper.
5. Place the chicken on a baking sheet lined with parchment paper and bake in the preheated oven for 20-25 minutes or until cooked through.
6. Serve with lemon wedges and fresh parsley on top.

LENTIL AND VEGETABLE SOUP

Made for: Dinner | Prep Time: 15 minutes | Total time: 30 | Servings: Crusty bread

Ingredients

- 1 cup of lentils, rinsed and drained
- 2 cups of vegetable broth
- 1 cup of diced carrots
- 1 cup of diced celery
- 1 cup of diced onion
- 2 cloves of garlic, minced
- 1 teaspoon of dried thyme
- Salt and pepper, to taste
- 2 tablespoons of olive oil

Instructions

1. In a large pot, heat the olive oil over medium heat. Add the onion, carrot, celery, and garlic and sauté for 5 minutes or until the vegetables are tender.
2. Stir in the lentils, vegetable broth, thyme, salt, and pepper. Bring to a boil, then reduce heat and simmer for 15-20 minutes or until the lentils are tender.
3. Serve with crusty bread on the side.

SHRIMP AND VEGETABLE SKEWERS

Made for: Dinner   *| Prep Time: 15 minutes | Total time: 30 | Servings: Lemon wedges, Fresh parsley, chopped*

Ingredients

- 1 lb of shrimp, peeled and deveined
- 2 cups of diced vegetables (such as bell peppers, onion, and zucchini)
- 2 cloves of garlic, minced
- 2 tablespoons of olive oil
- 2 tablespoons of lemon juice
- 1 teaspoon of dried oregano
- Salt and pepper, to taste

Instructions

1. Preheat grill to medium-high heat.
2. In a small bowl, mix together the olive oil, lemon juice, garlic, oregano, salt, and pepper.
3. Thread the shrimp and vegetables onto skewers and brush with the olive oil mixture.
4. Grill the skewers for 4-6 minutes per side or until the shrimp is cooked through and the vegetables are tender.
5. Serve with lemon wedges and fresh parsley on top.

VEGETABLE AND TOFU STIR FRY

Made for: Dinner | Prep Time: 15 minutes | Total time: 2 0 | Servings: Cooked rice

Ingredients

- 1 block of firm tofu, drained and cubed
- 2 cups of mixed vegetables (such as bell peppers, broccoli, and carrots)
- 2 cloves of garlic, minced
- 2 tablespoons of soy sauce
- 2 tablespoons of rice vinegar
- 1 teaspoon of sesame oil
- Salt and pepper, to taste
- 2 tablespoons of vegetable oil

Instructions

1. In a small bowl, mix together the soy sauce, rice vinegar, sesame oil, salt, and pepper.
2. Heat the vegetable oil in a large skillet or wok over high heat. Add the tofu and stir-fry for 2-3 minutes or until golden brown. Remove from skillet and set aside.
3. Add the vegetables and garlic to the skillet and stir-fry for 2-3 minutes or until tender-crisp.
4. Add the tofu and sauce to the skillet and stir-fry for another 1-2 minutes, or until the sauce is thickened and the tofu is heated through.
5. Serve over cooked rice.

GRILLED EGGPLANT AND TOMATO STACK

Made for: Dinner | Prep Time: 10 minutes | Total time: 2 0 | Servings: Fresh basil, chopped, Grated Parmesan cheese

Ingredients

- 2 large eggplants, sliced
- 2 large tomatoes, sliced
- 2 cloves of garlic, minced
- 2 tablespoons of olive oil
- 1 teaspoon of dried basil
- Salt and pepper, to taste

Instructions

1. Preheat grill to medium-high heat.
2. In a small bowl, mix together the olive oil, garlic, basil, salt, and pepper.
3. Brush the eggplant and tomato slices with the olive oil mixture.
4. Grill the eggplant and tomato slices for 2-3 minutes per side or until tender and slightly charred.
5. Assemble the eggplant and tomato slices in stacks and secure with a toothpick.
6. Serve with fresh basil and grated Parmesan cheese on top.

Note: In all these recipes, you can use vegetables that are low in FODMAPs, like kale, carrots, eggplants, and green beans.

Low Fodmap Vegetarian

Low-FODMAP vegetarian recipes are an excellent option for those following a low-FODMAP diet and vegetarian or vegan. These recipes are designed to be easy on the digestive system and perfect for those suffering from IBS or other digestive disorders. Not only do these recipes provide relief from symptoms, but they are also delicious and nutritious.

One of the benefits of a low FODMAP vegetarian diet is the variety of flavors and textures that can be achieved. From creamy curries to hearty casseroles, the options are endless. Imagine biting into a mouthwatering vegetable and quinoa casserole, bursting with the flavors of fresh vegetables and the nuttiness of quinoa. Or a savory tempeh chili with protein and the perfect balance of spices. These recipes will not only relieve symptoms but also inspire you to get creative in the kitchen and try new ingredients.

Not only do these recipes taste great, but they also offer numerous health benefits. A low FODMAP vegetarian diet is rich in fruits, vegetables, legumes, and whole grains, all important sources of fiber, vitamins, and minerals. Additionally, many low FODMAP vegetarian recipes are gluten-free, making them an excellent option for those with gluten sensitivities. By incorporating these recipes into your diet, you can enjoy all the benefits of a low FODMAP diet while also getting the nutrients your body needs.

In short, low-FODMAP vegetarian recipes are delicious, healthy, and easy to manage IBS and other digestive disorders. With a wide variety of flavors and ingredients, these recipes will provide relief from symptoms and inspire you to get creative in the kitchen.

SPINACH AND FETA STUFFED PORTOBELLO MUSHROOMS

Made for: Vegetarian | Prep Time: 10 minutes | Total time: 25 | Servings: Quinoa or rice

Ingredients

- 4 large portobello mushrooms
- 1 tbsp olive oil
- 1/4 tsp salt
- 1/4 tsp black pepper
- 1/2 cup crumbled feta cheese
- 1 cup fresh spinach

Instructions

1. Preheat the oven to 375F.
2. Clean the mushrooms with a damp cloth and remove the stems.
3. Brush the mushrooms with olive oil and sprinkle with salt and pepper.
4. In a separate bowl, mix the feta cheese and spinach.
5. Stuff the mushroom caps with the feta and spinach mixture.
6. Place the mushrooms on a baking sheet and bake for 20-25 minutes, or until the mushrooms are tender and the filling is heated through.

Notes: Be sure to remove the stems of the mushrooms before stuffing, as they contain high levels of FODMAPs.

ZUCCHINI NOODLES WITH AVOCADO PESTO

Made for: Vegetarian | Prep Time: 15 minutes | Total time: 25 | Servings: Grilled chicken or shrimp (optional)

Ingredients

- 2 medium zucchinis
- 1 avocado
- 1/4 cup chopped fresh basil
- 2 cloves of garlic
- 2 tbsp pine nuts
- 1/4 tsp salt
- 1/4 tsp black pepper
- 1/4 cup grated parmesan cheese
- 2 tbsp olive oil

Instructions

1. Spiralize the zucchini to create noodles.
2. In a food processor, combine the avocado, basil, garlic, pine nuts, salt, pepper, and parmesan cheese. Pulse until smooth.
3. Heat olive oil in a pan over medium heat. Add the zucchini noodles and sauté for 3-5 minutes or until tender.
4. Toss the zucchini noodles with the avocado pesto and serve.

Notes: Garlic is high in FODMAPs, so be sure to use only 2 cloves or omit it entirely.

EGGPLANT ROLLATINI

Made for: Vegetarian | Prep Time: 15 minutes | Total time: 40 | Servings: Quinoa or rice

Ingredients

- 1 large eggplant
- 1/4 tsp salt
- 1/4 tsp black pepper
- 1/2 cup ricotta cheese
- 1/4 cup grated parmesan cheese
- 1 cup fresh spinach
- 1/4 cup marinara sauce

Instructions

1. Preheat the oven to 375F.
2. Cut the eggplant into 1/4 inch slices and sprinkle with salt and pepper.
3. Mix the ricotta cheese, parmesan cheese, and spinach separately.
4. Spread a spoonful of the ricotta mixture on each slice of eggplant and roll it up, securing it with toothpicks if needed.
5. Place the rollatini in a baking dish and top with marinara sauce.
6. Bake for 30-35 minutes or until the eggplant is tender and the filling is heated.

SWEET POTATO AND BLACK BEAN ENCHILADAS

Made for: Vegetarian | Prep Time: 15 minutes | Total time: 35 | Servings: Guacamole or sour cream (optional)

Ingredients

- 2 medium sweet potatoes
- 1 can of black beans
- 1/4 cup diced onion
- 1/4 cup chopped bell pepper
- 1/4 tsp cumin
- 1/4 tsp chili powder
- 1/4 tsp salt
- 1/4 tsp black pepper
- 8 corn tortillas
- 1 cup enchilada sauce
- 1/4 cup grated cheddar cheese

Instructions

1. Preheat the oven to 375F.
2. Peel and dice the sweet potatoes and boil or steam until tender.
3. In a separate pan, sauté the onion and bell pepper until softened.
4. Mix the sweet potatoes, black beans, sautéed vegetables, cumin, chili powder, salt, and pepper.
5. Spread a spoonful of the sweet potato mixture on each tortilla and roll it up.
6. Place the enchiladas in a baking dish and top with enchilada sauce and cheese.
7. Bake for 20-25 minutes or until the enchiladas are heated, and the cheese is melted.

Notes: Onion and bell pepper are high in FODMAPs, so use a small amount or omit them entirely.

QUINOA AND BLACK BEAN BURGERS

Made for: Vegetarian | Prep Time: 10 minutes | Total time: 20 | Servings: Whole wheat buns, Lettuce and tomato

Ingredients

- 1 cup cooked quinoa
- 1 can of black beans
- 1/4 cup diced onion
- 1/4 cup chopped bell pepper
- 1/4 cup diced carrots
- 1 clove of garlic
- 1 egg
- 1/4 tsp cumin
- 1/4 tsp chili powder
- 1/4 tsp salt
- 1/4 tsp black pepper

Instructions

1. In a food processor, pulse the quinoa, black beans, onion, bell pepper, carrots, and garlic until well combined.
2. Transfer the mixture to a bowl and add the egg, cumin, chili powder, salt, and pepper. Mix well.
3. Form the mixture into four patties.
4. Heat a skillet over medium heat and cook the burgers for 3-5 minutes per side or until browned and cooked.
5. Serve the burgers on whole wheat buns with lettuce and tomato.

Notes: Onion and bell pepper are high in FODMAPs, so use a small amount or omit them entirely.

CAULIFLOWER AND CHICKPEA CURRY

Made for: Vegetarian | Prep Time: 10 minutes | Total time: 30 | Servings: Quinoa or rice

Ingredients

- 1 head of cauliflower
- 1 can chickpeas
- 1 diced onion
- 2 cloves of garlic
- 1 tbsp curry powder
- 1 tsp cumin
- 1/4 tsp salt
- 1/4 tsp black pepper
- 1 cup coconut milk

Instructions

1. Cut the cauliflower into small florets.
2. In a pan, sauté the onion and garlic until softened.
3. Add the cauliflower, chickpeas, curry powder, cumin, salt, and pepper to the pan. Sauté for a few minutes.
4. Pour in the coconut milk and bring to a simmer.
5. Let the curry simmer for 10-15 minutes or until the cauliflower is tender.
6. Serve the curry over quinoa or rice.

Notes: Onion and garlic are high in FODMAPs, so use a small amount or omit them entirely.

LENTIL AND SPINACH LASAGNA

Made for: Vegetarian | Prep Time: 20 minutes | Total time: 60 | Servings: Salad or garlic bread (optional)

Ingredients

- 1 cup cooked lentils
- 10 oz frozen spinach
- 1/2 cup ricotta cheese
- 1/4 cup grated parmesan cheese
- 1/4 tsp nutmeg
- 1/4 tsp salt
- 1/4 tsp black pepper
- 8 lasagna noodles
- 2 cups marinara sauce
- 1 cup grated mozzarella cheese

Instructions

1. Preheat the oven to 375F.
2. In a separate pan, sauté the frozen spinach until thawed and softened.
3. Mix the cooked lentils, sautéed spinach, ricotta cheese, parmesan cheese, nutmeg, salt, and pepper in a separate bowl.
4. Spread a thin layer of marinara sauce on the bottom of a 9x13-inch baking dish.
5. Place a layer of lasagna noodles on top of the sauce.
6. Spread a layer of the lentil and spinach mixture on top of the noodles, followed by another layer of marinara sauce.
7. Repeat the layering process until all the ingredients are used up, ending with a layer of marinara sauce on top.
8. Sprinkle the mozzarella cheese on top of the lasagna.
9. Cover the lasagna with foil and bake for 30 minutes. Remove the foil and bake for 20-25 minutes, until the cheese is golden brown and the lasagna is heated.
10. Let the lasagna cool for a few minutes before slicing and serving.

STUFFED BELL PEPPERS

Made for: Vegetarian | Prep Time: 15 minutes | Total time: 45 | Servings: Green salad

Ingredients

- 4 large bell peppers
- 1 cup cooked quinoa
- 1 can of black beans
- 1/4 cup diced onion
- 1/4 cup chopped bell pepper
- 1 clove of garlic
- 1/2 cup diced tomatoes
- 1 tsp cumin
- 1/4 tsp salt
- 1/4 tsp black pepper
- 1/4 cup grated cheddar cheese

Instructions

1. Preheat the oven to 375F.
2. Cut the tops off the bell peppers and remove the seeds.
3. In a pan, sauté the onion, bell pepper, and garlic until softened.
4. Mix the sautéed vegetables, quinoa, black beans, diced tomatoes, cumin, salt, and pepper.
5. Stuff the bell pepper with the quinoa and bean mixture.
6. Place the bell peppers in a baking dish and top with grated cheese.
7. Bake for 30-35 minutes or until the bell peppers are tender and the cheese is melted.
8. Serve the stuffed bell peppers with a green salad.

Notes: Onion and bell pepper are high in FODMAPs, so use a small amount or omit them entirely.

TOFU AND VEGETABLE STIR-FRY

Made for: Vegetarian | Prep Time: 15 minutes| Total time: 2 5 | Servings: Quinoa or rice

Ingredients

- 1 block of firm tofu
- 2 tbsp olive oil
- 1 diced onion
- 1 diced carrot
- 1 diced bell pepper
- 1 diced zucchini
- 2 cloves of garlic
- 1/4 cup soy sauce
- 1 tsp cornstarch
- 1/4 tsp black pepper

Instructions

1. Drain the tofu and press out the excess water. Cut the tofu into small cubes.
2. Heat the olive oil in a pan over medium-high heat. Add the onion, carrot, bell pepper, zucchini, and garlic. Sauté for 3-5 minutes or until the vegetables are tender.
3. Push the vegetables to one side of the pan and add the tofu to the other side. Cook for 3-5 minutes or until the tofu is browned.
4. Mix the soy sauce, cornstarch, and pepper in a small bowl.
5. Pour the soy sauce mixture over the vegetables and tofu. Cook for 1-2 minutes or until the sauce thickens.
6. Serve the stir-fry over quinoa or rice.

Notes: Onion and garlic are high in FODMAPs, so use a small amount or omit them entirely.

CHICKPEA AND SPINACH CURRY

Made for: Vegetarian *| Prep Time: 10 minutes | Total time: 30 | Servings: Quinoa or rice*

Ingredients

- 1 can chickpeas
- 1 diced onion
- 2 cloves of garlic
- 1 tbsp curry powder
- 1 tsp cumin
- 1/4 tsp salt
- 1/4 tsp black pepper
- 1 cup coconut milk
  2 cups fresh spinach

Instructions

1. In a pan, sauté the onion and garlic until softened.
2. Add the chickpeas, curry powder, cumin, salt, and pepper to the pan. Sauté for a few minutes.
3. Pour in the coconut milk and bring to a simmer.
4. Add the spinach to the pan and stir until it wilts.
5. Let the curry simmer for 10-15 minutes or until the chickpeas are tender.
6. Serve the curry over quinoa or rice.

Notes: Onion and garlic are high in FODMAPs, so use a small amount or omit them entirely.

BLACK BEAN AND SWEET POTATO TACOS

Made for: Vegetarian | Prep Time: 15 minutes | Total time: 2 5 | Servings:

Ingredients

- 2 medium sweet potatoes
- 1 can of black beans
- 1/4 cup diced onion
- 1/4 cup chopped bell pepper
- 1/4 tsp cumin
- 1/4 tsp chili powder
- 1/4 tsp salt
- 1/4 tsp black pepper
- 8 corn tortillas
- 1/4 cup grated cheddar cheese
- toppings of your choice (lettuce, tomato, salsa, guacamole, etc.)

Instructions

1. Peel and dice the sweet potatoes. Boil or steam them until tender.
2. In a separate pan, sauté the onion and bell pepper until softened.
3. Mix the cooked sweet potatoes, black beans, sautéed vegetables, cumin, chili powder, salt, and pepper.
4. Heat the tortillas in a pan or on a grill.
5. Place a spoonful of the sweet potato and black bean mixture on each tortilla.
6. Sprinkle grated cheese on top and add toppings of your choice.
7. Fold the tortilla in half and enjoy.

Notes: Onion and bell pepper are high in FODMAPs, so use a small amount or omit them entirely.

ROASTED VEGETABLE AND QUINOA SALAD

Made for: Vegetarian | Prep Time: 15 minutes | Total time: 45 | Servings: Arugula or mixed greens

Ingredients

- 2 cups diced vegetables of your choice (such as bell peppers, zucchini, eggplant, or onion)
- 2 tbsp olive oil
- 1 tsp herbs of your choice (such as oregano, thyme, rosemary)
- 1/4 tsp salt
- 1/4 tsp black pepper
- 1 cup cooked quinoa
- 2 tbsp balsamic vinegar
- 2 tbsp olive oil
- 1/4 tsp dijon mustard
- 1/4 tsp honey
- Salt and pepper to taste

Instructions

1. Preheat the oven to 425F.
2. Toss the diced vegetables with 2 tbsp of olive oil, herbs, salt, and pepper.
3. Spread the vegetables on a baking sheet and roast for 20-25 minutes or until tender and lightly browned.
4. Whisk together the balsamic vinegar, 2 tbsp of olive oil, dijon mustard, honey, salt, and pepper in a separate bowl.
5. Combine the cooked quinoa, roasted vegetables, and dressing in a large bowl. Toss to coat.
6. Serve the salad over a bed of arugula or mixed greens.

Note: Make sure to use vegetables that are low in FODMAPs for this recipe

LENTIL AND VEGETABLE SHEPHERD'S PIE

Made for: Vegetarian *| Prep Time: 15 minutes | Total time: 60 | Servings: Green salad*

Ingredients

- 1 cup lentils
- 3 cups vegetable broth
- 1 diced onion
- 1 diced carrot
- 1 diced celery
- 2 cloves of garlic
- 1 diced sweet potato
- 1 diced zucchini
- 1 diced bell pepper
- 1 tsp oregano
- 1 tsp thyme
- 1/4 tsp salt
- 1/4 tsp black pepper
- 2 cups mashed potatoes

Instructions

1. Preheat the oven to 375F.
2. In a pot, bring the lentils and vegetable broth to a boil. Reduce heat and let simmer for 20-25 minutes or until the lentils are tender.
3. In a separate pan, sauté the onion, carrot, celery, and garlic until softened.
4. Add the lentils to the pot with the sautéed vegetables, sweet potato, zucchini, bell pepper, oregano, thyme, salt, and pepper.
5. Let the mixture simmer for 10-15 minutes or until the vegetables are tender.
6. Transfer the lentil and vegetable mixture to a baking dish.
7. Spread the mashed potatoes over the top of the lentil mixture.
8. Bake for 20-25 minutes, or until the mashed potatoes are golden brown and the filling is heated through.
9. Serve the shepherd's pie with a green salad.

SPAGHETTI SQUASH AND PESTO

Made for: Vegetarian | Prep Time: 10 minutes| Total time: 45 | Servings: Green salad or garlic bread (optional)

Ingredients

- 1 spaghetti squash
- 1/2 cup prepared pesto
- 1/4 cup grated parmesan cheese
- salt and pepper to taste

Instructions

1. Preheat the oven to 375F.
2. Cut the spaghetti squash in half lengthwise and scoop out the seeds.
3. Place the squash halves on a baking sheet, cut side up, and season with salt and pepper.
4. Bake for 30-40 minutes or until the flesh is tender and easily shredded with a fork.
5. Once the squash is cool enough to handle, use a fork to shred the flesh into spaghetti-like strands.
6. Toss the spaghetti squash with pesto and grated parmesan cheese in a large bowl.
7. Serve immediately, garnishing with additional parmesan cheese if desired.

Notes: Pesto is typically made with basil, pine nuts, Parmesan cheese, and olive oil. Make sure to use a low-FODMAP pesto recipe or purchase a low-FODMAP pesto from the store.

VEGETABLE AND BEAN CHILI

Made for: Vegetarian | Prep Time: 15 minutes | Total time: 45 | Servings: Sour cream, grated cheese, or green onions (optional)

Ingredients

- 1 can of black beans
- 1 can of kidney beans
- 1 diced onion
- 2 cloves of garlic
- 1 diced bell pepper
- 1 diced zucchini
- 1 diced carrot
- 1 can diced tomatoes
- 1 tbsp chili powder
- 1 tsp cumin
- 1/4 tsp salt
- 1/4 tsp black pepper

Instructions

1. In a pan, sauté the onion, garlic, bell pepper, zucchini, and carrot until softened.
2. Add the diced tomatoes, chili powder, cumin, salt, and pepper to the pan. Sauté for a few minutes.
3. Add the black beans and kidney beans to the pan and stir until heated.
4. If desired, serve the chili with sour cream, grated cheese, or green onions.

Notes: Onion and garlic are high in FODMAPs, so use a small amount or omit them entirely.

QUINOA AND VEGETABLE BUDDHA BOWL

Made for: Vegetarian | Prep Time: 15 minutes | Total time: 2 5 | Servings: Avocado, green onions, or sesame seeds (optional)

Ingredients

- 1 cup cooked quinoa
- 1 diced bell pepper
- 1 diced zucchini
- 1 diced carrot
- 1 diced onion
- 2 cloves of garlic
- 1 tbsp olive oil
- 1 tsp soy sauce
- 1 tsp rice vinegar
- 1 tsp sesame oil
- salt and pepper to taste

Instructions

1. In a pan, sauté the bell pepper, zucchini, carrot, onion, and garlic in olive oil until softened.
2. Mix the soy sauce, rice vinegar, sesame oil, salt, and pepper in a small bowl.
3. Add the quinoa to the pan with the vegetables, and pour the sauce. Toss to coat.
4. Serve the Buddha bowl in bowls and garnish with avocado, green onions, or sesame seeds if desired.

Notes: Onion and garlic are high in FODMAPs, so use a small amount or omit them entirely.

VEGETABLE AND LENTIL CURRY

Made for: Vegetarian | Prep Time: 15 minutes | Total time: 45 | Servings: Rice or quinoa

Ingredients

- 1 cup dried green or brown lentils
- 3 cups water or vegetable broth
- 1 diced onion
- 2 cloves of garlic
- 1 diced sweet potato
- 1 diced carrot
- 1 diced bell pepper
- 1 diced zucchini
- 2 tbsp curry powder
- 1 tsp cumin
- 1 tsp turmeric
- 1/4 tsp salt
- 1/4 tsp black pepper
- 1 can of coconut milk

Instructions

1. Rinse the lentils in a pot with water or vegetable broth. Bring to a boil, then reduce heat and let simmer for 20-25 minutes or until the lentils are tender.
2. In a separate pan, sauté the onion and garlic until softened.
3. Add the sweet potato, carrot, bell pepper, zucchini, curry powder, cumin, turmeric, salt, and pepper to the pan. Sauté for a few minutes.
4. Stir in the cooked lentils and coconut milk, and bring to a simmer.
5. Let the curry simmer for 10-15 minutes or until the vegetables are tender.
6. Serve the curry over rice or quinoa.

Notes: Onion and garlic are high in FODMAPs, so use a small amount or omit them entirely.

VEGETABLE AND TOFU CURRY

Made for: Vegetarian | Prep Time: 15 minutes | Total time: 2 5 | Servings: Rice or quinoa

Ingredients

- 1 block of firm tofu
- 2 tbsp olive oil
- 1 diced onion
- 2 cloves of garlic
- 1 diced sweet potato
- 1 diced carrot
- 1 diced bell pepper
- 1 diced zucchini
- 2 tbsp curry powder
- 1 tsp cumin
- 1/4 tsp salt
- 1/4 tsp black pepper
- 1 can of coconut milk

Instructions

1. Drain the tofu and press out the excess water. Cut the tofu into small cubes.
2. Heat the olive oil in a pan over medium-high heat. Add the onion, garlic, sweet potato, carrot, bell pepper, and zucchini. Sauté for 3-5 minutes or until the vegetables are tender.
3. Stir in the curry powder, cumin, salt, pepper, and sauté for a few more minutes.
4. Add the tofu and coconut milk to the pan, and bring to a simmer.
5. Let the curry simmer for 5-10 minutes or until the tofu is heated and the sauce has thickened.
6. Serve the curry over rice or quinoa.

Notes: Onion and garlic are high in FODMAPs, so use a small amount or omit them entirely.

VEGETABLE AND CHICKPEA CURRY

Made for: Vegetarian | Prep Time: 15 minutes | Total time: 2 5 | Servings: Rice or quinoa

Ingredients

- 1 can chickpeas
- 2 tbsp olive oil
- 1 diced onion
- 2 cloves of garlic
- 1 diced sweet potato
- 1 diced carrot
- 1 diced bell pepper
- 1 diced zucchini
- 2 tbsp curry powder
- 1 tsp cumin
- 1/4 tsp salt
- 1/4 tsp black pepper
- 1 can of coconut milk

Instructions

1. In a pan, heat the olive oil over medium-high heat. Add the onion and garlic, and sauté until softened.
2. Stir in the sweet potato, carrot, bell pepper, zucchini, and sauté for 3-5 minutes or until the vegetables are tender.
3. Add the chickpeas, curry powder, cumin, salt, and pepper to the pan, and sauté for a few more minutes.
4. Pour in the coconut milk and bring the mixture to a simmer.
5. Let the curry simmer for 10-15 minutes or until the sauce thickens and the vegetable tender.
6. Serve the curry over rice or quinoa.

Notes: Onion and garlic are high in FODMAPs, so use a small amount or omit them entirely.

EGGPLANT AND TOMATO PARMESAN

Made for: Vegetarian | Prep Time: 15 minutes | Total time: 40 | Servings: Pasta or garlic bread (optional)

Ingredients

- 1 large eggplant
- 1 cup all-purpose flour
- 2 eggs
- 1 cup breadcrumbs
- 1/4 tsp salt
- 1/4 tsp black pepper
- 1 cup marinara sauce
- 1 cup grated mozzarella cheese
- 1/4 cup grated parmesan cheese

Instructions

1. Preheat the oven to 375F.
2. Slice the eggplant into 1/2-inch thick rounds.
3. In a shallow dish, mix the flour, salt, and pepper.
4. In another shallow dish, beat the eggs.
5. In a third shallow dish, mix the breadcrumbs.
6. Dip each eggplant round into the flour mixture, then into the eggs, and finally into the breadcrumbs.
7. Place the breaded eggplant rounds on a baking sheet and bake for 20-25 minutes or until golden brown and tender.
8. In a baking dish, spread the marinara sauce over the bottom.
9. Place the baked eggplant rounds on top of the marinara sauce.
10. Sprinkle mozzarella cheese and parmesan cheese over the top.
11. Bake for 10-15 minutes or until the cheese is melted and bubbly.
12. Serve the eggplant parmesan with pasta or garlic bread if desired.

VEGETABLE AND PANEER CURRY

Made for: Vegetarian | Prep Time: 15 minutes | Total time: 2 5 | Servings: Rice or quinoa

Ingredients

- 1 cup diced paneer
- 2 tbsp olive oil
- 1 diced onion
- 2 cloves of garlic
- 1 diced sweet potato
- 1 diced carrot
- 1 diced bell pepper
- 1 diced zucchini
- 2 tbsp curry powder
- 1 tsp cumin
- 1/4 tsp salt
- 1/4 tsp black pepper
- 1 can of coconut milk

Instructions

1. In a pan, heat the olive oil over medium-high heat. Add the onion and garlic, and sauté until softened.
2. Stir in the sweet potato, carrot, bell pepper, zucchini, and sauté for 3-5 minutes or until the vegetables are tender.
3. Add the paneer, curry powder, cumin, salt, and pepper to the pan, and sauté for a few more minutes.
4. Pour in the coconut milk and bring the mixture to a simmer.
5. Let the curry simmer for 10-15 minutes or until the sauce thickens and the vegetable tender.
6. Serve the curry over rice or quinoa.

Notes: Onion and garlic are high in FODMAPs, so use a small amount or omit them entirely.

VEGETABLE AND BEAN ENCHILADAS

Made for: Vegetarian *| Prep Time: 15 minutes | Total time: 45 | Servings: Sour cream or guacamole (optional)*

Ingredients

- 1 can of black beans
- 1 can of kidney beans
- 1 diced onion
- 2 cloves of garlic
- 1 diced bell pepper
- 1 diced zucchini
- 1 diced carrot
- 1 can red enchilada sauce
- 8-10 corn tortillas
- 1 cup grated cheese

Instructions

1. Preheat the oven to 375F.
2. In a pan, sauté the onion, garlic, bell pepper, zucchini, and carrot until softened.
3. Add the black beans, kidney beans, enchilada sauce, salt, and pepper to the pan and stir until heated.
4. Spread a little bit of the bean mixture on each tortilla and roll them up.
5. Place the rolled-up tortillas in a baking dish and pour the remaining bean mixture on top.
6. Sprinkle grated cheese over the top.
7. Bake for 20-25 minutes or until the cheese is melted and the enchiladas are heated.
8. Serve the enchiladas with sour cream or guacamole if desired.

Notes: Onion and garlic are high in FODMAPs, so use a small amount or omit them entirely.

VEGETABLE AND TOFU STIR FRY

Made for: Vegetarian | Prep Time: 15 minutes | Total time: 2 5 | Servings: Rice or quinoa

Ingredients

- 1 block of firm tofu
- 2 tbsp vegetable oil
- 1 diced onion
- 2 cloves of garlic
- 1 diced bell pepper
- 1 diced carrot
- 1 diced zucchini
- 1 diced broccoli
- 2 tbsp soy sauce
- 1 tsp rice vinegar
- 1 tsp sesame oil
- salt and pepper to taste

Instructions

1. Drain the tofu and press out the excess water. Cut the tofu into small cubes.
2. Heat the vegetable oil in a pan over medium-high heat. Add the onion, garlic, bell pepper, carrot, zucchini, and broccoli. Sauté for 3-5 minutes or until the vegetables are tender.
3. Mix the soy sauce, rice vinegar, sesame oil, salt, and pepper in a small bowl.
4. Add the tofu to the pan with the vegetables, and pour the sauce. Toss to coat.
5. Serve the stir-fry over rice or quinoa.

Notes: Onion and garlic are high in FODMAPs, so use a small amount or omit them entirely.

VEGETABLE AND CASHEW CURRY

Made for: Vegetarian | Prep Time: 15 minutes | Total time: 2 5 | Servings: Rice or quinoa

Ingredients

- 1 cup cashews
- 2 tbsp olive oil
- 1 diced onion
- 2 cloves of garlic
- 1 diced sweet potato
- 1 diced carrot
- 1 diced bell pepper
- 1 diced zucchini
- 2 tbsp curry powder
- 1 tsp cumin
- 1/4 tsp salt
- 1/4 tsp black pepper
- 1 can of coconut milk

Instructions

1. In a pan, heat the olive oil over medium-high heat. Add the onion and garlic, and sauté until softened.
2. Stir in the sweet potato, carrot, bell pepper, zucchini, and sauté for 3-5 minutes or until the vegetables are tender.
3. Add the cashews, curry powder, cumin, salt, and pepper to the pan, and sauté for a few more minutes.
4. Pour in the coconut milk and bring the mixture to a simmer.
5. Let the curry simmer for 10-15 minutes or until the sauce thickens and the vegetable tender.
6. Serve the curry over rice or quinoa.

Notes: Onion and garlic are high in FODMAPs, so use a small amount or omit them entirely.

VEGETABLE AND QUINOA CASSEROLE

Made for: Vegetarian | Prep Time: 15 minutes | Total time: 45 | Servings: Green salad or garlic bread (optional)

Ingredients

- 1 cup quinoa
- 2 cups water or vegetable broth
- 1 diced onion
- 2 cloves of garlic
- 1 diced sweet potato
- 1 diced carrot
- 1 diced bell pepper
- 1 diced zucchini
- 1 diced broccoli
- 1 cup grated cheese
- 1/4 tsp salt
- 1/4 tsp black pepper

Instructions

1. Preheat the oven to 375F.
2. Rinse the quinoa in a pot with water or vegetable broth. Bring to a boil, then reduce heat and let simmer for 15-20 minutes or until the quinoa is tender.
3. In a separate pan, sauté the onion and garlic until softened.
4. Add the sweet potato, carrot, bell pepper, zucchini, broccoli, salt, pepper, and sauté for a few minutes.
5. Stir in the cooked quinoa and grated cheese.
6. Transfer the mixture to a baking dish and bake for 25-30 minutes or until the cheese is melted and bubbly.
7. Serve the casserole with a green salad or garlic bread if desired.

Notes: Onion and garlic are high in FODMAPs, so use a small amount or omit them entirely.

VEGETABLE AND SEITAN CURRY

Made for: Vegetarian | Prep Time: 15 minutes | Total time: 2 5 | Servings: Rice or quinoa

Ingredients

- 1 cup diced seitan
- 2 tbsp olive oil
- 1 diced onion
- 2 cloves of garlic
- 1 diced sweet potato
- 1 diced carrot
- 1 diced bell pepper
- 1 diced zucchini
- 2 tbsp curry powder
- 1 tsp cumin
- 1/4 tsp salt
- 1/4 tsp black pepper
- 1 can of coconut milk

Instructions

1. In a pan, heat the olive oil over medium-high heat. Add the onion and garlic, and sauté until softened.
2. Stir in the sweet potato, carrot, bell pepper, zucchini, and sauté for 3-5 minutes or until the vegetables are tender.
3. Add the seitan, curry powder, cumin, salt, and pepper to the pan, and sauté for a few more minutes.
4. Pour the coconut milk and bring the mixture to a simmer.
5. Let the curry simmer for 10-15 minutes or until the sauce thickens and the vegetable tender.
6. Serve the curry over rice or quinoa.

Notes: Onion and garlic are high in FODMAPs, so use a small amount or omit them entirely. Seitan is not suitable for a gluten-free diet.

VEGETABLE AND TEMPEH CHILI

Made for: Vegetarian | Prep Time: 15 minutes | Total time: 40 | Servings: Sour cream or green onion (optional)

Ingredients

- 1 cup diced tempeh
- 1 diced onion
- 2 cloves of garlic
- 1 diced bell pepper
- 1 diced zucchini
- 1 diced carrot
- 1 diced sweet potato
- 1 can diced tomatoes
- 1 can of kidney beans
- 1 tbsp chili powder
- 1 tsp cumin
- 1/4 tsp salt
- 1/4 tsp black pepper
- 1 cup grated cheese

Instructions

1. In a pan, sauté the onion, garlic, bell pepper, zucchini, and carrot until softened.
2. Add the tempeh, diced tomatoes, kidney beans, chili powder, cumin, salt, and pepper to the pan.
3. Simmer for 15-20 minutes or until the vegetables are tender and the chili is heated.
4. Serve the chili with grated cheese, sour cream, or green onion if desired.

Notes: Onion and garlic are high in FODMAPs, so use a small amount or omit them entirely.

These are general recipes that may need adjustments for personal taste and dietary restrictions. Also, all the ingredient measurements are approximate and can be adjusted according to personal preference.

Low Fodmap Sides Dishes

Low FODMAP dishes are an excellent option for those with IBS or other digestive sensitivities, as they are designed to be easy on the digestive system. These 15 low-FODMAP side dishes are not only delicious and satisfying but they are also packed with nutrients and flavor. From grilled fish and zucchini fries to creamed spinach and pan-fried radicchio, these recipes inspire you to get creative in the kitchen and make mealtime more enjoyable. Whether you're looking for a quick and easy weeknight dinner or a special occasion side dish, these recipes are sure to please. So get ready to satisfy your cravings and nourish your body with these mouthwatering low-FODMAP side dishes!

ROASTED VEGETABLES

Made for: Sides Dishes| Prep Time: 10 minutes| Total time: 40 | Servings: 0 4 people

Ingredients

- 1 zucchini, diced
- 1 eggplant, diced
- 1 red bell pepper, diced
- 1 yellow bell pepper, diced
- 2 tbsp olive oil
- Salt and pepper, to taste

Instructions

1. Preheat the oven to 375°F (190°C).
2. Toss the diced vegetables with olive oil, salt, and pepper in a large bowl.
3. Spread the vegetables on a baking sheet and roast for 30-40 minutes or until tender and slightly browned.
4. Serve warm as a side dish.

Notes: You can add other low-FODMAP vegetables like asparagus, broccoli, or cauliflower.

QUINOA SALAD

Made for: Sides Dishes| Prep Time: 10 minutes | Total time: 20 | Servings: 0 4 people

Ingredients

- 1 cup quinoa, cooked
- 1/4 cup diced tomatoes
- 1/4 cup diced cucumber
- 1/4 cup chopped bell pepper
- 2 tbsp olive oil
- 2 tbsp lemon juice
- Salt and pepper, to taste

Instructions

1. In a large bowl, combine the cooked quinoa, diced tomatoes, cucumber, and bell pepper.
2. Whisk together the olive oil, lemon juice, salt, and pepper in a small bowl.
3. Pour the dressing over the quinoa mixture and toss to combine.
4. Serve chilled as a side dish.

Notes: You can add other low-FODMAP vegetables like asparagus, broccoli, or cauliflower.

CAULIFLOWER RICE

Made for: Sides Dishes| Prep Time: 10 minutes | Total time: 20 | Servings: 0 4 people

Ingredients

- 1 head of cauliflower, grated
- 2 tbsp olive oil
- Salt and pepper, to taste

Instructions

1. Heat the olive oil in a large skillet over medium heat.
2. Add the grated cauliflower and season with salt and pepper.
3. Cook for about 10 minutes until the cauliflower is tender and lightly browned.
4. Serve as a side dish.

Notes: You can add other low-FODMAP vegetables like asparagus, broccoli, or cauliflower.

GARLIC-INFUSED MASHED POTATOES

Made for: Sides Dishes| Prep Time: 15 minutes | Total time: 30 | Servings: 0 4 people

Ingredients

- 4 medium potatoes, peeled and diced
- 1/4 cup unsweetened almond milk
- 2 tbsp olive oil
- Salt and pepper, to taste

Instructions

1. Boil the diced potatoes in a pot of salted water for about 20 minutes or until tender.
2. Drain the potatoes and return them to the pot.
3. Add the almond milk and olive oil and mash the potatoes until smooth.
4. Season with salt and pepper to taste.
5. Serve as a side dish.

Notes: You can also add other low FODMAP ingredients like chives or parsley for added flavor.

GREEN BEANS WITH LEMON AND ALMONDS

Made for: Sides Dishes| Prep Time: 10 minutes | Total time: 20 | Servings: 0 4 people

Ingredients

- 1 lb green beans, trimmed
- 2 tbsp olive oil
- 2 tbsp lemon juice
- 1/4 cup sliced almonds
- Salt and pepper, to taste

Instructions

1. Bring a pot of salted water to a boil.
2. Add the green beans and cook for about 5 minutes or until tender.
3. Drain the green beans and transfer them to a bowl.
4. Toss the green beans with olive oil, lemon juice, almonds, salt, and pepper.
5. Serve as a side dish.

Notes: You can add other low-FODMAP vegetables like asparagus, broccoli, or cauliflower.

BAKED SWEET POTATO FRIES

Made for: Sides Dishes | Prep Time: 10 minutes | Total time: 30 | Servings: 0 4 people

Ingredients

- 2 sweet potatoes, peeled and cut into wedges
- 2 tbsp olive oil
- Salt and pepper, to taste

Instructions

1. Preheat the oven to 425°F (220°C).
2. Toss the sweet potato wedges with olive oil, salt, and pepper in a large bowl.
3. Spread the wedges on a baking sheet and bake for 25-30 minutes, until crispy and tender.
4. Serve as a side dish.

Notes: You can also add other low FODMAP herbs and spices like rosemary or paprika for added flavor.

GRILLED ASPARAGUS

Made for: Sides Dishes| Prep Time: 10 minutes| Total time: 10 | Servings: 0 4 people

Ingredients

- 1 lb asparagus, trimmed
- 2 tbsp olive oil
- Salt and pepper, to taste

Instructions

1. Preheat the grill to medium-high heat.
2. Toss the asparagus with olive oil, salt, and pepper in a large bowl.
3. Grill the asparagus for about 5 minutes per side or until tender and lightly charred.
4. Serve as a side dish.

Notes: You can add other low FODMAP herbs and spices like garlic powder or lemon zest for added flavor.

CABBAGE SLAW

Made for: Sides Dishes | Prep Time: 10 minutes | Total time: 10 | Servings: 0 4 people

Ingredients

- 1/2 head of green cabbage, thinly sliced
- 1/4 cup diced bell pepper
- 1/4 cup diced cucumber
- 2 tbsp apple cider vinegar
- 2 tbsp olive oil
- Salt and pepper, to taste

Instructions

1. In a large bowl, combine the sliced cabbage, bell pepper, and cucumber.
2. Whisk together the apple cider vinegar, olive oil, salt, and pepper in a small bowl.
3. Pour the dressing over the cabbage mixture and toss to combine.
4. Let the slaw sit for at least 10 minutes to allow the flavors to meld.
5. Serve as a side dish.

Notes: You can add other low FODMAP vegetables like grated carrot or radicchio.

ROASTED BRUSSELS SPROUTS

Made for: Sides Dishes| Prep Time: 10 minutes | Total time: 30 | Servings: 0 4 people

Ingredients

- 1 lb Brussels sprouts, trimmed and halved
- 2 tbsp olive oil
- Salt and pepper, to taste

Instructions

1. Preheat the oven to 375°F (190°C).
2. Toss the Brussels sprouts in a large bowl with olive oil, salt, and pepper.
3. Spread the Brussels sprouts on a baking sheet and roast for 25-30 minutes or until tender and slightly browned.
4. Serve as a side dish.

Notes: You can add other low FODMAP herbs and spices like garlic powder or lemon zest for added flavor.

CARROT AND GINGER PUREE

Made for: Sides Dishes| Prep Time: 10 minutes | Total time: 25 | Servings: 0 4 people

Ingredients

- 2 lbs carrots, peeled and chopped
- 2 tbsp fresh ginger, grated
- 2 tbsp unsweetened almond milk
- Salt and pepper, to taste

Instructions

1. Bring a pot of salted water to a boil.
2. Add the chopped carrots and ginger and cook for about 15 minutes or until tender.
3. Drain the carrots and ginger and transfer them to a blender or food processor.
4. Add the almond milk and puree until smooth.
5. Season with salt and pepper to taste.
6. Serve as a side dish.

Notes: You can add other low FODMAP ingredients like butter or olive oil for added richness

LEMON AND HERB GRILLED FISH

Made for: Sides Dishes| Prep Time: 10 minutes | Total time: 10 | Servings: 0 4 people

Ingredients

- 4 fish fillets (such as salmon or cod)
- 2 tbsp olive oil
- 2 tbsp lemon juice
- 1 tbsp fresh thyme, chopped
- 1 tbsp fresh parsley, chopped
- Salt and pepper, to taste

Instructions

1. Preheat the grill to medium-high heat.
2. Mix the olive oil, lemon juice, thyme, parsley, salt, and pepper in a small bowl.
3. Brush the fish fillets with the olive oil mixture.
4. Grill the fish for about 4-5 minutes per side or until cooked through.
5. Serve as a side dish.

Notes: You can add other low FODMAP herbs and spices like rosemary or garlic powder for added flavor.

BAKED ZUCCHINI FRIES

Made for: Sides Dishes| Prep Time: 10 minutes | Total time: 30 | Servings: 0 4 people

Ingredients

- 2 zucchinis, cut into wedges
- 1/2 cup gluten-free breadcrumbs
- 2 tbsp grated Parmesan cheese
- 2 tbsp olive oil
- Salt and pepper, to taste

Instructions

1. Preheat the oven to 425°F (220°C).
2. In a shallow dish, mix the breadcrumbs and Parmesan cheese.
3. Toss the zucchini wedges in a large bowl with olive oil, salt, and pepper.
4. Dip the wedges into the breadcrumb mixture, pressing to coat.
5. Place the wedges on a baking sheet and bake for 25-30 minutes or until crispy and tender.
6. Serve as a side dish.

Notes: You can also add other low FODMAP herbs and spices like rosemary or paprika for added flavor.

PAN-FRIED RADICCHIO

Made for: Sides Dishes| Prep Time: 10 minutes | Total time: 10 | Servings: 0 4 people

Ingredients

- 1 head of radicchio, thinly sliced
- 2 tbsp olive oil
- 2 tbsp balsamic vinegar
- Salt and pepper, to taste

Instructions

1. Heat the olive oil in a large skillet over medium heat.
2. Add the radicchio and cook for about 5 minutes or until wilted and lightly browned.
3. Remove from heat and toss with balsamic vinegar, salt, and pepper.
4. Serve as a side dish.

Notes: You can add other low FODMAP herbs and spices like garlic powder or lemon zest for added flavor.

CREAMED SPINACH

Made for: Sides Dishes| Prep Time: 10 minutes | Total time: 20 | Servings: 0 4 people

Ingredients

- 1 lb spinach, washed and stemmed
- 2 tbsp unsweetened almond milk
- 2 tbsp grated Parmesan cheese
- 1 tbsp olive oil
- Salt and pepper, to taste

Instructions

1. In a large skillet, heat the olive oil over medium heat.
2. Add the spinach and cook for about 5 minutes or until wilted.
3. Remove from heat and transfer to a blender or food processor.
4. Add the almond milk and Parmesan cheese and puree until smooth.
5. Season with salt and pepper to taste.
6. Serve as a side dish.

Notes: You can add other low FODMAP ingredients like cream cheese or sour cream for added richness.

Low Fodmap Dessert

Desserts are often thought of as indulgent treats that we   enjoy on special occasions or as a reward for a job well done. But for those of us following a low FODMAP diet, finding a dessert that is both delicious and safe to eat can be a challenge. That's why I'm excited to share with you a recipe for a dessert th   at is not only low FODMAP, but also irresistibly delicious.

As someone who has struggled with digestive issues for years, I know firsthand how difficult it can be to find desserts that don't leave me feeling bloated and uncomfortable. But when I discovered this recipe, it was a game changer. Not only is it easy to make, but it's also made with simple, wholesome ingredients that won't upset your stomach.

The best part about this dessert, though, is that it doesn't sacrifice flavor for digestibility. Each bit   e is a perfect balance of sweetness and richness, with just the right amount of crunch. It's the kind of dessert that you'll want to savor slowly, letting the flavors and textures dance on your tongue.

But what really sets this dessert apart is the way   it makes you feel. When you take a bite, it's like a warm hug for your taste buds, lifting your spirits and making you feel comforted and happy. It's the perfect treat for those moments when you need a little pick   -me -up, or when you just want to indulge in   something sweet without the worry of how it will affect your digestion.

So go ahead, give this recipe a try. I promise you won't be disappointed. In fact, I think it might just become your new go-to dessert, something you'll want to share with all your friends and family, whether they follow a low FODMAP diet or not. Because when a dessert is this good, everyone should get to enjoy it.

BLUEBERRY CRUMBLE

Made for: Desserts | Prep Time: 15 minutes | Total time: 4 5 | Servings: vanilla ice cream or whipped cream

Ingredients

- 2 cups blueberries
- 1/4 cup granulated sugar
- 1/4 cup brown sugar
- 1/2 cup gluten-free flour
- 1/2 cup rolled oats
- 1/2 cup unsalted butter, chilled and cubed

Instructions

1. Preheat the oven to 375°F.
2. In a mixing bowl, combine the blueberries, granulated sugar, and brown sugar.
3. In a separate mixing bowl, combine the gluten-free flour, rolled oats, and butter. Mix until the mixture resembles coarse crumbs.
4. Transfer the blueberry mixture to a 9-inch baking dish.
5. Sprinkle the crumb mixture on top of the blueberries.
6. Bake for 35-40 minutes or until the topping is golden brown and the blueberries are bubbly.
7. Serve warm with vanilla ice cream or whipped cream.

CHOCOLATE MOUSSE

Made for: Desserts| Prep Time: 10 minutes | Total time: 30 | Servings: whipped cream or berries

Ingredients

- 8 oz. dark chocolate, chopped
- 1/2 cup heavy cream
- 2 large eggs, separated
- 1/4 cup granulated sugar

Instructions

1. In a heatproof bowl, combine the chopped chocolate and cream.
2. Set the bowl over a saucepan of simmering water and stir until the chocolate is melted and the mixture is smooth.
3. Remove the bowl from the heat and let it cool for a few minutes.
4. In a separate mixing bowl, beat the egg yolks and sugar until thick and pale.
5. In another mixing bowl, beat the egg whites until stiff peaks form.
6. Gently fold the egg yolk mixture into the cooled chocolate mixture.
7. Gently fold the egg whites into the chocolate mixture.
8. Spoon the mousse into glasses or ramekins and refrigerate for at least 30 minutes.
9. Serve chilled with whipped cream or berries.

APPLE CRISP

Made for: Desserts| Prep Time: 15 minutes | Total time: 45 | Servings: vanilla ice cream or whipped cream

Ingredients

- 4 cups peeled and sliced apples
- 1/4 cup granulated sugar
- 1/4 cup brown sugar
- 1/2 cup gluten-free flour
- 1/2 cup rolled oats
- 1/2 cup unsalted butter, chilled and cubed

Instructions

1. Preheat the oven to 375°F.
2. In a mixing bowl, combine the apples, granulated sugar, and brown sugar.
3. In a separate mixing bowl, combine the gluten-free flour, rolled oats, and butter. Mix until the mixture resembles coarse crumbs.
4. Transfer the apple mixture to a 9-inch baking dish.
5. Sprinkle the crumb mixture on top of the apples.
6. Bake for 35-40 minutes or until the topping is golden brown and the apples are tender.
7. Serve warm with vanilla ice cream or whipped cream.

LEMON BARS

Made for: Desserts | Prep Time: 20 minutes | Total time: 1 hour | Servings: powdered sugar

Ingredients

- 1 cup gluten-free flour
- 1/2 cup powdered sugar
- 1/2 cup unsalted butter, chilled and cubed
- 2 large eggs
- 1/2 cup granulated sugar
- 2 tbsp lemon zest
- 1/4 cup fresh lemon juice

Instructions

1. Preheat the oven to 350°F.
2. In a mixing bowl, combine the gluten-free flour, powdered sugar, and butter. Mix until the mixture resembles coarse crumbs.
3. Press the mixture into a 9-inch square baking dish lined with parchment paper.
4. Bake for 15-20 minutes or until the crust is golden brown.
5. In a separate mixing bowl, beat the eggs, granulated sugar, lemon zest, and lemon juice.
6. Pour the mixture over the crust and bake for an additional 15-20 minutes or until the filling is set.
7. Let the bars cool completely before cutting into squares.
8. Dust with powdered sugar before serving.

CHOCOLATE CHIP COOKIES

Made for: Desserts| Prep Time: 15 minutes | Total time: 25 | Servings:

Ingredients

- 1 1/4 cup gluten-free flour
- 1 tsp baking powder
- 1/2 tsp baking soda
- 1/2 cup unsalted butter, at room temperature
- 1/2 cup granulated sugar
- 1/4 cup brown sugar
- 1 large egg
- 1 tsp vanilla extract
- 1/2 cup semi-sweet chocolate chips

Instructions

1. Preheat the oven to 350°F.
2. In a mixing bowl, combine the gluten-free flour, baking powder, and baking soda.
3. In a separate mixing bowl, beat the butter, granulated sugar, and brown sugar until creamy.
4. Beat in the egg and vanilla extract.
5. Slowly add the flour mixture to the butter mixture and mix until well combined.
6. Stir in the chocolate chips.
7. Drop spoonfuls of the dough onto a baking sheet lined with parchment paper.
8. Bake for 12-15 minutes or until the edges are golden brown.
9. Let the cookies cool on the baking sheet for a few minutes before transferring them to a wire rack to cool completely.

STRAWBERRY SORBET

Made for: Desserts| Prep Time: 10 minutes| Total time: 2 hours | Servings:

Ingredients

- 2 cups fresh strawberries, hulled
- 1/2 cup granulated sugar
- 1/4 cup water
- 1 tbsp fresh lemon juice

Instructions

1. In a blender or food processor, puree the strawberries until smooth.
2. In a small saucepan, combine the sugar and water. Bring to a boil over medium heat, stirring until the sugar is dissolved.
3. Remove the pan from the heat and let the syrup cool.
4. Stir in the strawberry puree and lemon juice.
5. Pour the mixture into a 9-inch square baking dish and freeze for 1 hour.
6. Stir the mixture with a fork to break up any ice crystals.
7. Freeze for an additional 1 hour or until firm.
8. Scoop the sorbet into bowls and serve.

RICE PUDDING

Made for: Desserts| Prep Time: 10 minutes | Total time: 4 0 | Servings:

Ingredients

- 1 cup cooked white rice
- 2 cups almond milk
- 1/4 cup granulated sugar
- 1 tsp vanilla extract
- 1/4 tsp ground cinnamon
- 1/4 cup raisins (optional)
- For serving: cinnamon, nutmeg, or whipped cream

Instructions

1. In a medium saucepan, combine the cooked rice, almond milk, sugar, vanilla extract, and ground cinnamon.
2. Bring the mixture to a boil over medium heat, then reduce the heat to low and simmer for 25-30 minutes, or until the pudding thickens, stirring occasionally.
3. If desired, stir in the raisins during the last 5 minutes of cooking.
4. Remove the pudding from the heat and let it cool for a few minutes.
5. Serve warm or chilled, topped with a sprinkle of cinnamon, nutmeg, or whipped cream.

CHOCOLATE PUDDING

Made for: Desserts| Prep Time: 10 minutes | Total time: 20 | Servings: whipped cream or berries

Ingredients

- 2 cups almond milk
- 1/4 cup cornstarch
- 1/4 cup granulated sugar
- 2 oz. dark chocolate, chopped
- 1 tsp vanilla extract

Instructions

1. In a medium saucepan, whisk together the almond milk, cornstarch, and sugar.
2. Heat the mixture over medium heat, stirring constantly, until it begins to thicken.
3. Remove the pan from the heat and stir in the chopped chocolate and vanilla extract until the chocolate is melted and the pudding is smooth.
4. Let the pudding cool for a few minutes.
5. Serve warm or chilled, topped with whipped cream or berries.

PEACH COBBLER

Made for: Desserts| Prep Time: 15 minutes | Total time: 45 | Servings: vanilla ice cream or whipped cream

Ingredients

- 2 cups peeled and sliced peaches
- 1/4 cup granulated sugar
- 1/4 cup brown sugar
- 1/2 cup gluten-free flour
- 1/2 cup rolled oats
- 1/2 cup unsalted butter, chilled and cubed

Instructions

1. Preheat the oven to 375°F.
2. In a mixing bowl, combine the peaches, granulated sugar, and brown sugar.
3. In a separate mixing bowl, combine the gluten-free flour, rolled oats, and butter. Mix until the mixture resembles coarse crumbs.
4. Transfer the peach mixture to a 9-inch baking dish.
5. Sprinkle the crumb mixture on top of the peaches.
6. Bake for 35-40 minutes or until the topping is golden brown and the peaches are tender.
7. Serve warm with vanilla ice cream or whipped cream.

BANANA BREAD

Made for: Desserts| Prep Time: 15 minutes | Total time: 1 hour | Servings:

Ingredients

- 1 1/2 cup gluten-free flour
- 1 tsp baking powder
- 1/2 tsp baking soda
- 1/2 cup unsalted butter, at room temperature
- 1/2 cup granulated sugar
- 1/4 cup brown sugar
- 2 large eggs
- 1 tsp vanilla extract
- 3 ripe bananas, mashed

Instructions

1. Preheat the oven to 350°F.
2. In a mixing bowl, combine the gluten-free flour, baking powder, and baking soda.
3. In a separate mixing bowl, beat the butter, granulated sugar, and brown sugar until creamy.
4. Beat in the eggs and vanilla extract.
5. Stir in the mashed bananas.
6. Slowly add the flour mixture to the banana mixture and mix until well combined.
7. Pour the batter into a 9x5 inch loaf pan lined with parchment paper.
8. Bake for 50-60 minutes or until a toothpick inserted into the center comes out clean.
9. Let the bread cool in the pan for 10 minutes before transferring it to a wire rack to cool completely.

MANGO SORBET

Made for: Desserts | Prep Time: 10 minutes | Total time: 2 hours | Servings:

Ingredients

- 2 cups frozen mango
- 1/2 cup granulated sugar
- 1/4 cup water
- 1 tbsp fresh lime juice

Instructions

1. In a blender or food processor, puree the frozen mango until smooth.
2. In a small saucepan, combine the sugar and water. Bring to a boil over medium heat, stirring until the sugar is dissolved.
3. Remove the pan from the heat and let the syrup cool.
4. Stir in the mango puree and lime juice.
5. Pour the mixture into a 9-inch square baking dish and freeze for 1 hour.
6. Stir the mixture with a fork to break up any ice crystals.
7. Freeze for an additional 1 hour or until firm.
8. Scoop the sorbet into bowls and serve.

TAPIOCA PUDDING

Made for: Desserts| Prep Time: 10 minutes| Total time: 20 | Servings: berries or whipped cream

Ingredients

- 1 cup small pearl tapioca
- 2 cups almond milk
- 1/4 cup granulated sugar
  1 tsp vanilla extract

Instructions

1. In a medium saucepan, combine the tapioca, almond milk, sugar, and vanilla extract.
2. Bring the mixture to a boil over medium heat, then reduce the heat to low and simmer for 15-20 minutes, or until the pudding thickens, stirring occasionally.
3. Remove the pudding from the heat and let it cool for a few minutes.
4. Serve warm or chilled, topped with berries or whipped cream.

BROWNIES

Made for: Desserts | Prep Time: 15 minutes | Total time: 30 | Servings: *powdered sugar or whipped cream*

Ingredients

- 1 cup gluten-free flour
- 1/2 cup unsweetened cocoa powder
- 1/2 tsp baking powder
- 1/2 cup unsalted butter, melted
- 1/2 cup granulated sugar
- 1/4 cup brown sugar
- 2 large eggs
- 1 tsp vanilla extract
- 1/2 cup semi-sweet chocolate chips

Instructions

1. Preheat the oven to 350°F.
2. In a mixing bowl, combine the gluten-free flour, cocoa powder, and baking powder.
3. In a separate mixing bowl, beat together the melted butter, granulated sugar, and brown sugar.
4. Beat in the eggs and vanilla extract.
5. Slowly add the flour mixture to the butter mixture and mix until well combined.
6. Stir in the chocolate chips.
7. Pour the batter into a 8x8 inch baking pan lined with parchment paper.
8. Bake for 20-25 minutes or until a toothpick inserted into the center comes out clean.
9. Let the brownies cool in the pan for 10 minutes before transferring them to a wire rack to cool completely.
10. Dust with powdered sugar or serve with whipped cream before serving.

PECAN PIE

Made for: Desserts | Prep Time: 15 minutes | Total time: 1 hour | Servings: whipped cream

Ingredients

- 1/2 cup gluten-free flour
- 1/2 cup granulated sugar
- 1/4 cup brown sugar
- 1/4 cup unsalted butter, melted
- 1 tsp vanilla extract
- 2 large eggs
- 1 cup chopped pecans

Instructions

1. Preheat the oven to 350°F.
2. In a mixing bowl, combine the gluten-free flour, granulated sugar, and brown sugar.
3. Stir in the melted butter, vanilla extract, and eggs until well combined.
4. Stir in the chopped pecans.
5. Pour the mixture into a 9-inch pie dish.
6. Bake for 40-45 minutes or until the filling is set.
7. Let the pie cool completely before serving.
8. Serve with whipped cream.

PINEAPPLE UPSIDE-DOWN CAKE

Made for: Desserts| Prep Time: 15 minutes | Total time: 45 | Servings:

Ingredients

- 1/2 cup unsalted butter, at room temperature
- 1/2 cup granulated sugar
- 1 large egg
- 1 tsp vanilla extract
- 1/2 cup gluten-free flour
- 1/2 tsp baking powder
- 1/2 cup unsweetened pineapple juice
- 1/4 cup brown sugar
- 1 can pineapple slices, drained
- Maraschino cherries (optional)

Instructions

1. Preheat the oven to 350°F.
2. In a mixing bowl, beat the butter and granulated sugar together until creamy.
3. Beat in the egg and vanilla extract.
4. In a separate mixing bowl, combine the gluten-free flour and baking powder.
5. Slowly add the flour mixture to the butter mixture and mix until well combined.
6. Spread the brown sugar in the bottom of a 9-inch round cake pan.
7. Place the pineapple slices on top of the brown sugar.
8. If desired, place a cherry in the center of each pineapple slice.
9. Pour the batter over the pineapple slices.
10. Bake for 30-35 minutes or until a toothpick inserted into the center comes out clean.
11. Let the cake cool for 5 minutes before inverting it onto a serving plate.
12. Serve warm or at room temperature.

Note:

For these recipes, you may use substitutions for ingredients that may not comply with low-FODMAP diet.

Always check the ingredients and their portion if it's suitable for low-FODMAP diet.

You can also add or subtract ingredients according to your preference.

It's important to note that some individuals may have different tolerances for certain ingredients, even if they are considered to be low-FODMAP. It's always best to consult with a healthcare professional or a registered dietitian for personalized advice. Additionally, it's important to be mindful of portion sizes when following a low-FODMAP diet, as consuming large amounts of a low-FODMAP food may still cause symptoms.

Conclusion

The low FODMAP diet efficiently manages the signs associated with IBS or other digestive conditions. This book offers an extensive 30-day meal plan (BONUS) that includes various meals, breakfast, lunch vegetarian, side meals, and desserts that contain a low amount of FODMAPs. The recipes are tasty, simple to cook, and will let you feel more relaxed and enjoy food.

The main takeaway from this guidebook is that it's possible to have a balanced and satisfying diet while adhering to the low FODMAP diet. By choosing high-quality, nutritious foods and avoiding high-FODMAP food that may cause problems, you can effectively control your symptoms and enhance your overall quality of life.

One effective strategy that will assist you in reaching the goals you want to achieve is, to begin with, minor adjustments. Instead of revamping your entire diet at once, you can begin by making minor adjustments to your food choices. For instance, you can swap those high FODMAP fruits with lower FODMAP alternatives or make use of low FODMAP marinades and sauces. When you gradually make minor adjustments, you'll be able to transition to the Low FODMAP diet faster and will be more likely to stick to it for the long haul.

Overall, this book is an excellent source for anyone who wants to improve their digestion by following the low FODMAP diet. With a broad selection of tasty and easy-to-prepare recipes, this book will indeed become an indispensable appliance in your kitchen. Start playing around with low FODMAP recipes then you'll marvel at how better you'll feel. Have fun cooking!

Photos credits:

www.flickr.com

www.pexels.com

www.pxhere.com

www.needpix.com

www.rawpixel.com

Made in the USA
Monee, IL
17 April 2023

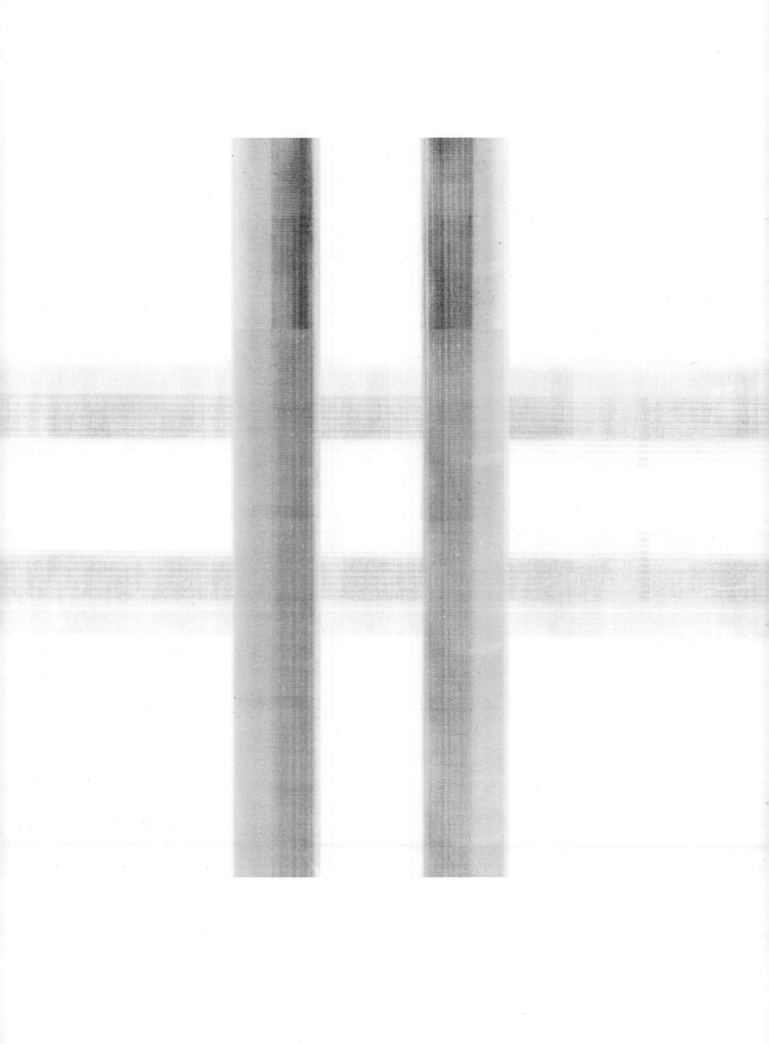